The King's Men

The King's Men

Tom McCarthy

PLUTO PRESS

London

First published 1990 by Pluto Press
345 Archway Road, London N6 5AA

Copyright © 1990 Tom McCarthy

British Library Cataloguing in Publication Data
McCarthy, Tom, *1925–*
    The King's men.
    1. World War 2. Western European
    campaigns. Army operations by Great
    Britain. Army. Grenadier Guards
    I. Title
    940.54'21

    ISBN 0–7453–0310–2 hb
    ISBN 0–7453–0414–1 pb

Typeset by Stanford Desktop Publishing Services, Milton Keynes
Printed in Great Britain

Contents

For Joan

The diamond in my life

Foreword

When I volunteered for the Grenadier Guards in 1944 I had no inkling that I would witness the world's best-known trial and see at first hand the suffering and devastation a few megalomaniac madmen could wreak on a country and its inhabitants.

It is difficult to imagine what it would have been like in Britain if our civilisation had been destroyed – no government or administration, no shelter, no food, no transport. The security and comfort of the old, familiar way of life replaced by chaos, fear and confusion. It was just such a situation that I was to experience when, as a volunteer for special duties, I landed in Germany in 1945.

Many of those who had survived the bombing and the ravages of invading armies must have wondered whether survival was worth the effort. Their entire world had collapsed and been replaced by unrelenting misery. They found what shelter they could in holes in the rubble of their destroyed cities. Their days were spent scavenging for food and fuel or queueing for hours at soup kitchens or one of the few shops with food to sell, hoping that stocks would last out until their turn came.

Disease was rife: the water supplies were polluted, the pipes damaged and unrepaired. In summer the air was foetid with the stench of dead bodies still entombed under the rubble and littering the surrounding countryside. Only the rats were well fed.

The normal currency counted for little. Barter and the black market thrived; cigarettes, chocolate and soap assumed unbelievable values. A single cigarette would buy the services of a pretty young woman for the night. That one cigarette would not be smoked, it would buy food on the black market the next day.

To try to escape the chaos was futile. The transport system was in ruins and the fares beyond the means of all but the rich. You could wait days for a train that never arrived, and the stations were crowded with people trying to get away. At the same time the roads from the east were choked with thousands upon thousands of refugees trying to get in. A never ending stream of destitute humanity pushing what was left of their lives in battered carts, prams – anything on wheels. Among these victims of war were desperate men who would stop at nothing to escape and survive. Some operated in groups and were prepared to kill anyone who got in their way. Twice I almost fell victim to their ruthlessness – one more killing mattered very little to men who had witnessed wholesale slaughter and brutality. This was Germany in 1945.

This book was written for two reasons: first, having witnessed the suffering of people like you and me and the victors' attempts to bring those responsible to justice, I saw the sheer futility of war. Secondly, people and nations have short memories. I want them to remember.

1

The Summons

It was one of those murky London mornings – the now familiar smells of smoke and cordite still lingered on the damp September air as I stood by the open window trying to wake up. The half-smoked fag hanging from my lips tasted crappy as I gazed at the scene outside with bleary eyes; the autumn mist had combined with the smoke from chimneys and burning buildings to draw a veil over the wide view of London that we usually had from our flat in the tenement block. I could only just make out some of the allotments on the once grassed area in front of the flats, each one with its rows of sooty cabbages and potatoes. It was one of those mornings after the night before, if you get me – I had been boozing with some mates until late and there had been the usual night raid and I was short of sleep. The Jerries were still trying to bury us, and they hadn't succeeded so I assumed they would be back again that night to have another try.

I was still standing there half asleep, smoking and drinking a cup of lukewarm tea (there was more sterilised milk in it than tea and it tasted even worse than the fag) when I heard the steps of the postman coming along the balcony. The footsteps stopped outside the front door; the unmistakable sound of an envelope falling from the letter-box flap woke me up in a hurry. I went into the hallway and there on the doormat lay a long, brown, official-looking envelope; from where I was standing I could see the letters OHMS and my stomach screwed up into a knot. I bent down to pick it up. My hands were clammy and shaking and I felt sick and short of breath. I knew it was for me. Four years of bombing hadn't had the same effect on me as this brown envelope was having right then! A month had gone by since the four of us, Harry Hazel, my cousins Charlie and Tommy Green and I, had jumped on the back of that lorry to Euston Road and enlisted. Ever since that day I had listened for the postman with apprehension; it had been a spur of the moment impulse by the four of us, all fed up and out of work, to join up. At the time it had seemed a good idea, and now the moment I had never believed would come had arrived.

I had been called up.

I ripped open the envelope and read the letter. I was to report to the Guards Depot at Caterham in two days time. By now my nerves were having their usual effect on my guts and I had to make a beeline to the khazi for a crap. As I sat there I remember thinking 'Blimey, I don't even know where Caterham is!' The other thought that occupied me just then was what I was going to say to my Dad. I hadn't told him that I had signed up. I felt he had enough on his plate without being faced with this any sooner than necessary. Having left most of my innards down the pan I made another pot of tea and lit another fag to calm myself down. As I sat there in the quiet flat pondering the situation, the battered old tin alarm clock ticking away what was left of my time in civvy street, I wondered if my mates had got their marching orders too.

I thought back to the day the four of us had so lightheartedly rolled into the recruiting office, joking about how drunk we would get on the King's Shilling. I remembered the enormous redcap sergeant with the red nose, bristling waxed moustache and a back as straight as an ironing board. His voice hadn't encouraged argument as he invited us to follow him. 'This way gentlemen please. Put that cigarette out.'

He had escorted us to a large gymnasium where medicals were being held. Round the hall were screens on castors arranged to form cubicles and as we sat down on a low wooden bench near the door we saw blokes walking into and out of the cubicles naked; some were carrying their belongings with them, while others dumped them on the floor outside the screens and collected them again as they moved on to the next cubicle. As the sergeant disappeared back to his desk in the entrance hall so our cheerfulness reasserted itself. Ignorant sods that we were, we had a good laugh at the sight of the poor unfortunates trying to hide their privates with cupped hands or clothes as they moved around the hall, but as it dawned on us that we were about to suffer the same indignities we suddenly didn't find it such a lark. When it became obvious that we were expected to provide a specimen we warned Harry, well known for his ability to down more pints than most, not to fill the specimen bottle to the top. We settled the question as to who was to go first by playing 'Odd Man Out' with our hands. I lost, and grumbling that it was a bloody fix, started to strip off; to save my blushes the other three stripped off too. We all stood there naked, our skins as white as snow, hiding our embarrassment behind grins that were as wide as our ears were apart. Despite the poverty and at times near starvation the four of us had endured in the slums, we were taller than average even though we were as skinny as only 18 year olds can be. Harry was the tallest, he was 6ft 2ins, and always looked every inch of that as he held himself very upright. He spoke slowly and had a dry sense of humour which appealed to me. He had learned to box in his time in the army cadets, so people who knew him didn't mess him about. The shortest of us was Charlie, but even he was 5ft 10ins; he was the Clark Gable type, with black curly hair. He was the joker of the pack and could keep people laughing until the cows came home. Tommy, his brother, was two inches taller and as fair as Charlie was dark. Although he was the youngest he didn't suffer fools gladly and people soon learned not to play him up either. As for me, I was just a shade under 6ft, round faced and sporting a short haircut, later known as a crew cut. The three regarded me as something approaching the fount of all wisdom – an undeserved title – because my insatiable reading habit had given me a wide general knowledge. There was a strong bond between us. Charlie and Tommy were cousins, of course, but we had all grown up in the Bunk, London's most notorious slum[1] and we had known each other all our lives; the fact that we had moved to different parts of Islington made no difference.

'Try a little harder', said the white coated doctor. I noticed his officer's army jacket hanging on a peg nearby.

'I am unable to go, sir.'

'Get a drink of water, and make sure you cover the bottom of the specimen bottle!'

'Yes sir.' By straining at the leash success came, half into the bottle and half on the floor.

'Next.'

The three of us were herded round the hall like sheep in a sheep dip, following each other around, classless, naked and unashamed. As we waited our turn we were treated to snippets of conversation from behind the screens.

'Any social diseases?' I heard one doctor ask.

'Only me sister, she's on the game!' came the reply from a wide boy. I could see the doctor's face in the crack between the material and the screen. He wore a pince-nez and had heard it all before.

'Cough.'...'Next.'

As we shuffled around I looked up. There was an air raid on at the time and through the glass skylight I saw a buzz bomb pass overhead. I remember thinking 'All these questions and carryings on and red tape to see if there was enough life in us to pass muster when we could all, doctors and recruits, be blown to kingdom come in a single moment.' There was plenty of life in us though, frozen as we were, as we moved ever nearer to the door at the end and out. We were rubber stamped at the finish and given a number.

'What did you make of that? 'Ere Charlie, did you see that guy covered in 'air all over his body, even 'is cupped 'ands couldn't 'ide it all, talk abaht a stallion!'

'Say, 'ave yer seen me socks anywhere, lads?'

'You're wearin' 'em!'

'Gawd 'elp us I'm in a right two and eight, what a bloody caper.'

As we were dressing, Charlie, the last of the four of us to finish, appeared crestfallen, he looked white.

'You alright Charlie?'

'Didn't make it', he said quietly.

'You've got ter be kiddin'!', said Tommy, one leg in his trousers and the other half way there.

'Nah, straight up', replied Charlie. 'I've got this bad ear see, perforated eardrum 'e says.'

'Do me a favour Charlie, what bad eardrum? You've got ter be kiddin mate!'

' 'Onest, Boysie, I got it because ol' Trumpy clouted me round the ear'ole when I was at school. You remember 'im, the thin streak of piss!', replied Charlie bitterly.

Only then did it dawn on us that he wasn't kidding.

'Blimey, what a turn up for the books!', mumbled Harry as we ambled along Euston Road towards St Pancras. 'Anyway there's always the pick an' shovel brigade Charlie, they'll take anyone s'long as they're still breathin'!'

'Very funny', retorted Charlie, not amused.

'Sorry mate, only tryin' ter help.'

The three of us tried to console Charlie as we made our way home, past bombed out buildings, stepping over piles of rubble, bombed churches with spires looking towards heaven for help and piles of soggy sandbags. Not that we noticed – we had our own problems just then – but it wasn't long before another hitch in our plans appeared.

The four of us had planned to stick together and join the same regiment, the Duke of Cornwall's Light Infantry. Why we had chosen that particular regiment I can't remember. It was probably my idea, stemming from my scanty knowledge of that beautiful county gained on a visit a few years earlier. It soon became obvious that only Harry had been assigned to that regiment, and he was as happy as a sand boy.

'See what I mean lads, they recognise class', smirked the ex-army cadet.

Tommy broke the news that he had been put in the RASC. I then told them what had happened to me.

As the attestation officer dropped the height peg of the measuring bar on the top of my head as I stood against the wall, he asked 'Would you like to go into the Guards?'

'Not really', I had replied. 'My mates and I want to join the Duke of Cornwall's Light Infantry.'

'Sorry', said the officer, 'we only have vacancies left for the Guards.'

I paused for a bit, not knowing what to do and thinking 'Blimey, they must have lost a lot of men!'

'O.K. I'll give it a try. What regiment will I be in?'

'The Grenadiers.'

'The Grenadier Guards', I thought as I made for the door, 'that's the lot that stands outside the Palace.'

When we discovered that all four of us were going different ways we were really fed up and were unusually quiet as we shuffled along York Way, sharing a fag between us. The walk back to the Bunk was a much more sombre and depressed journey than the one the four of us had taken earlier in the day. Whatever the future held we would have to face it alone, without the comfort of each other's friendship.

By the time we reached Finsbury Park it was opening time and into the nearest boozer, the Durham, we went and spent the rest of our cash in drinking the shocks of the day into oblivion.

I woke next morning with a thick head and the pressing problem of how I was going to get my attestation papers signed. I didn't dare to ask Dad in case he refused. In any case I felt I couldn't ask him to sign a paper which effectively increased my chances of being snuffed out. As I was walking along Seven Sisters Road later that morning I ran into Mickey Davies, an old school mate who had joined the Royal Navy and was home on leave. It was good to see him. He insisted we went and had a drink together. Mickey was good looking, with brown wavy hair and a grin which showed a row of good, even white teeth like the Macleans toothpaste advert.

'You'll 'ave ter stand the drinks then, Mickey. I'm stony broke after last night.'

'S'all right Boysie', he replied with a grin, 'what abaht last night?'

We pushed open the door of the Finsbury Park Tavern and sauntered to the bar. As we waited for our drinks I told him about the four of us, how our plans had collapsed and how I had ended up in the Grenadiers, and now had the problem of breaking the news to Mum and Dad and of getting the attestation papers signed.

The silence lasted a minute or two as Mickey downed the first few mouthfuls of his beer. Then he said 'Let's ask my stepdad to sign 'em for yer. 'E'll do it, no bovver.'

'You sure?' Wiping the froth from my mouth with my sleeve.

'Yeah, sure', replied Mickey, 'we'll go along this evenin', I'll meet yer at Turnpike Tube, seven o'clock suit yer?'

'Yeah. You sure he'll sign?' I said.

'No problem' replied Mickey 'you sure you want 'im ter sign?!'

I returned to the flat to collect the papers which I had hidden under the lino in our bedroom. No one was in so I scarpered as fast as I could before any awkward questions could be asked. Only when I was well away from the flat did I relax.

Soon after seven that evening Mickey and I walked up Turnpike Lane, bumping into people and scratching our faces on untrimmed hedges in the murk of the blackout. Under the railway bridges just before St Mary's Church it was pitch black and we ran the gauntlet of dripping water and pigeon droppings. Once on the level we soon came to the turning where Mickey's stepdad lived.

The stairs up to the first floor flat where the old boy lived were even darker than it had been outside and I hung on to the back of Mickey's coat as we stumbled up the creaking staircase. Once on the landing he pushed open a door into a room dimly lit by gaslight.

"Ello Dad. 'Ow yer doin'?" Mickey greeted the old boy.

"Ello Mickey, my old son, you on leave, boy?"

'This is Boysie. 'E wants you ter sign 'is call up papers. 'E's going in the Grenadiers', said Mickey, never one to waste words.

The old man held his hand out for the blue sheets of paper. He was a nice bloke with a round, jovial face and bright blue eyes topped by close cut grey hair. His beaming smile drew lines on a ruddy face that had seen more salt in its time than Saxa's, for he had spent many years in first the Royal Navy then the Merchant Navy. He had travelled all over the world and had tattoos on his arms to prove it. He wasn't all that tall, about 5ft 8ins, but he was stocky, built like a pocket battleship. A real old sweat. He was even called Sam.

After looking long and hard at me he turned to the papers, reading them carefully through steel-rimmed specs balanced precariously on the end of his red nose. The room was silent but for the hissing of the gas mantle on the wall.

An air raid was on and I could hear the throbbing sound of a doodlebug going over. Two had fallen on some houses nearby a few nights earlier and had left death and destruction where they landed and windowless houses on either side. At last Sam broke the silence, questioning me on why I wanted to join up, and why I hadn't asked Dad to sign the papers, and so on.

He hesitated and questioned me again, warning me what I would be letting myself in for. Only when he was sure in his own mind that I really meant to join up one way or another did he agree to sign. After what seemed an age he got out a battered, ink stained pen, with one of those steel nibs that could be changed, a bottle of Stephenson's ink and carefully signed his name along the dotted line. Then I relaxed, letting out a long hiss of air and glancing at Mickey in relief. The formalities completed, Sam stood up straight again, shook my hand firmly with both of his and wished me all the luck in the world.

'Thanks, Sam', I said gratefully.

As soon as we decently could we said goodbye and clattered down the creaking staircase into the blackout and made for the nearest pub. We celebrated our success over a pint of beer. All I had to do now was to tell Mum and Dad.

Much later, when I had been in the Army some time, lying soaking wet in the pouring rain trying to keep my bren gun dry, I thought of Sam and mentally nodded in agreement with his words of wisdom and experience.

Mum and Dad had gone to bed by the time I got home and I was glad to put off telling them what I had done for a few hours. Next morning though, I could put it off no longer. 'Dad', I said, trying to sound nonchalant and failing.

'Yus, Boysie.'

'Dad – I'm...I've joined up.'

Silence.

'You what?'

'I've joined up...the Grenadiers.'

'You must be bleedin' daft!' He exploded, while Mum, cool as a cucumber, said very little as she poured the tea from the chipped brown teapot. To save an argument I agreed. 'Yes, I'm bloody daft, stupid and out of my mind!'

There was heavy silence while he looked at me. His face was creased with anxiety and a suspicion of pride as he said, 'Look after yerself, son.'

'Yeah, course, Dad', I said, relieved that he had accepted it so quickly.

'Who signed yer papers for yer, 'cos I know I didn't!', he said after a while.

'Mickey Davies's stepdad – you know, the old sailor, lives over 'ornsey 'igh Street. I didn't want to ask you – knew you'd refuse', I replied, risking a grin.

'Dead right, I would 'ave', said Dad.

The call up papers gave me a couple of days to get myself organised. I ran into Mickey again and arranged to meet him the day before I left for Caterham. We decided to meet at Euston.

On the day we arranged to meet I hopped onto a 14 bus and booked to Euston, having my ticket punched by a very smart and attractive clippie. She was a right glamour puss and looked just like the girl in the Max Factor advert. 'Fares, pleeze', she called as she came slowly down the aisle from seat to seat, swinging her hips, 'Any more fares pleeze? Any more fares?'

'Euston darlin'', I said eyeing her up and down as she punched my ticket, which she took from a hand ticket rack and clipped in an old fashioned machine, her leather change bag slung over her shoulder by a brown leather strap. The sunlight through the webbing on the windows made a pattern on her jacket as she gave me my change. The change chinked, the ticket punch dinged and the bell rang – all she needed were bells on her toes!

I jumped off to the sound of the clippie's voice calling 'Ewstun, Ewstun Stashun' and crossed the long drive up to the gloomy Doric columns of the huge old entrance arch, passing on the way one of the more memorable London war memorials. It made you think.

The concourse and Hardwick's classical style hall were swarming with people, most of them in uniform. All were on their way to somewhere else, loaded up with kitbags, cases and holdalls. I picked my way through the khaki, navy and air force blue, my eyes homing in on likely looking matelots – viz Mickey. I stopped to light up a fag, my last, and gazed over the busy scene. I strolled to a kiosk for more fags.

'Ten Weights 'n a box of matches please. 'Ere Lady, 'ave yer seen a tall good lookin' sailor' in these parts?'

'If I 'ad, you'd be the last to know' retorted the brunette behind the counter.

'Ask a silly question' I thought as I moved away. I hung around among the steam of arriving and departing engines for about 20 minutes. The time passed quickly enough – I was happy eyeing the talent, my hands in pockets, and my eyes screwed up against the smoke which curled up from the fag in the corner of my mouth. I was comfortable and relaxed, leaning up against a pillar, trilby tilted forward in the style I had seen so often in the films. I reckon I could have been done for sus, no trouble.

Mickey finally turned up, sneaking up behind me and tapping me on the shoulder. 'Wotcher, Boysie', he grinned, looking great in his sailor's uniform, 'let's go fer a tea and a wad at the Church Army canteen.'

'I can't mate, I'm not in uniform.'

'Doesn't matter, got yer papers?'

'Yeah.'

'Show 'em those and yer railway warrant'

I fished them out of my pocket and checked them. Armed with this proof of my qualifications for a cuppa and a sandwich we set forth, jumping over kitbags, cases and other paraphernalia in our way. We reached the hut on the green in front of the station which housed the Church Army's tea shop. The tea and wads were being served by old girls with big smiles and nods of approval. Their gentle middle-class manners must have been welcome to the weary and no doubt homesick young conscripts who wandered in there. The atmosphere inside the hut was thick and the blue grey wisps of smoke hung in wraiths in the corners and across the ceiling just like a fog. I showed my papers to the smiling lady behind the counter who responded with an even broader smile and a nod. I looked round me as we waited for our turn to be served. There were some nice looking girls in ATS uniform sitting in one corner. We were soon eyeing them up.

'Sausage roll luv', and a pound out of the till', I quipped. The smile disappeared.

'Sorry missus – only joking luv' I assured her – I didn't want to get slung out before I'd had my tea and wad. We moved over to sit near the uniformed glamour and talked about the old days as well as smiling at the girls until Mickey had to leave.

Once on my own I set to work to chat up one of the ATS birds in the corner. It didn't take long. A few minutes later I joined their group and soon landed a good looking brunette who was whiling away a couple of hours before catching a train north. We made for a pub nearby and chatted over a half pint each – all I could afford by now. I was fascinated by the baggy uniform hat perched on her shining brown hair. Strolling back to Euston to see her onto her train after an hour or so, we made all those promises on parting that are never kept. It was dark by then and I grabbed her round her waist as we stumbled back along Euston Road in the gloom, narrowly missing being minced by a bus that drove by too close for comfort. A few kisses and cuddles in a quiet corner and then it was time to go. Brief laughter as our hats got tangled in the clinch and then she was gone.

I didn't sleep at all the night before I had to leave for Caterham. I got up with my mouth feeling full of gunge; it was good to get rid of the bad taste with a scalding cup of tea. The nicotine and wallop I had consumed the evening before had given me a thumping head and my bloodshot eyes felt like little gritted marbles as I squinted out of screwed up eyelids to read the travel instructions. I collected some bits and pieces I thought I would need and searched round for something to carry them in, eventually finding an old small attache case of thick brown covered cardboard. 'That'll do', I thought, as I crammed in a pair of socks. Spotting some of Mum's rock cakes in the kitchen, I put a couple in the case too before snapping shut the lid. I thought I might be needing a bit of home comfort by the end of the day.

As I stood in the kitchen sipping my second cup of tea and sucking at the last dregs of a Woodbine a letter dropped through the letterbox. It was for me. 'What the hell now', I thought, as I tore open the official looking envelope. It was from the income tax office. I read it through gradually focusing but still bloodshot eyeballs – couldn't understand it – so screwed it up and threw it on the fire. 'Everyone seems ter be after yer money', I thought. Having disposed of the taxman I turned again to the pressing problem of what to take with me.

A buzz bomb throbbed its way overhead and I willed it on, on over the sea where it would do no harm. I went out onto the balcony and waved it on with my hand, swearing at the bloody thing to keep the fire in its backside still burning and not to stop. A silence followed by a distant crump of an explosion told me it hadn't made it as far as the sea. My life seemed suddenly to have been taken over by outside forces and I couldn't get rid of the knot of tension in my midriff. I felt oddly breathless as I changed into my best navy serge suit, then plastered my hair into centre parting submission with a liberal helping of brilliantine from the 3d green tin from Woolies – not yer actual Brylcreem but better than the cooking fat we used when broke.

Packing completed, I scrounged a dollar from Dad, who had come in just in time, enough for a pint and a packet of fags – I'd only got a bob or so left after the socialising of the day before.

At last it was time to go.

'See yer', I called without looking back, as I walked to the front door. It had always been 'So long', never 'Goodbye' in our family, and on this occasion it would have hurt too much – seemed too final. I slammed the front door and whistled as I walked along the balcony and clattered down the stone stairs, kidding myself I was cool and in charge. I wasn't, I was keyed up inside and choked at leaving. I galloped out of the estate, wondering when – and if – I would ever see the gaunt block of red brick flats again. I must have looked like an escaping prisoner as I walked fast – my nose pointing towards the tube station, looking neither right nor left, only slowing down when I reached that part of the Great North Road we call Archway Road. Heavily loaded lorries hurtled down the gradient towards the Archway, knocking me about with their slipstream. They were a lot slower across the road where they ground and shuddered up the hill. One set my teeth on edge as the driver clashed the gears and I could see him mouthing curses as he wrestled with the gear lever. Preoccupied as I was, I jumped on a passing tram. 'Sod it', I thought, 'tube's better.' So I jumped off again before I got clobbered for a fare I couldn't afford.

'London Bridge, mate. Ta guv.' Having tucked the ticket safe in my breast pocket I lit another fag as I stood on the escalator. I exhaled, trying to blow a smoke ring and winking at a blonde on the upside staircase, a smashing looking creature with a page boy hair style. She grinned back. If my journey hadn't been necessary, I'd have climbed over to join her. I pulled hard on my cigarette, watching the gap between me and her back view getting ever bigger. Just before she reached the top she turned and I saluted her with my raised brown attache case, as she disappeared. I tightened my grip on the case and stepped off the escalator and down the windy passage to the platform. I felt grown up, a new sense of responsibility inside me had taken over. This was IT. ' 'Ere comes Flash Gordon on 'is way to Mars. London Bridge first stop.' I stepped into the tube train and off the space-ship roared down into the black hole of the tunnel towards Tufnell Park.

London Bridge was crowded with commuters and memories – hop-pickers' specials, Tattenham Corner specials on Derby Day. I jostled with pinstriped and bowlerhatted city gents and neatly dressed secretaries complete with gloves and hats. I swaggered over to the ticket collector. 'Caterham please, mate.' I hoped I was pronouncing the place right – I'd never heard of it until the call up papers arrived. I waved the railway warrant in front of his 'mince pies'. The old bloke scrutinised the warrant and eyed me up and down. 'Platform 4, there's one in 20 minutes', he nodded and winked as he folded the warrant and handed it back.

'Ta mate' – my nose and stomach guided me towards the station buffet bar.

'Let's have a cuppa tea Missus, please.' The woman behind the bar looked like she'd make a good sparring partner for a boxer, so I reckoned I'd better say 'please'. Her arms were like York hams, large and round and she'd a flat nose that would have looked better on a prize fighter. Her small eyes looked right through me as her deep voice boomed 'Anyfing else son?' She slammed the cup on the counter.

'You got any fruit cake, Missus?'

She waddled off to reach under the glass container and – wouldn't you know it – worked me a corner bit! I always ended up with the corner bits. I retired to a neutral corner and a slop-ridden table. With one eye on the clock I tackled the dry corner of the cake and washed it down with the tea. Having finished both, I just had time to get a paper before the train left. '*News Chronicle*, please.'

'Sorry, none left', says a little charmer behind the counter.

'Oh well, not ter worry.' I shrugged and walked out and onto the platform. Suddenly I wanted to be alone, so I walked down to the far end of the platform – I wanted to think yet I didn't want to think – my mind was ticking over like a timekeeper's watch. Looking back down the platform I saw a group of young blokes obviously heading for the same destination but I remained where I was, independent and doing my own thing to the last. Life in the Bunk made you that way, but it didn't stop me being mildly curious about them all the same.

At last the train clanked in and I grabbed a corner seat in a musty smelling carriage almost next to the guard's van. A couple and their children followed me in and I asked them whether the train was going to Caterham – the trouble was I couldn't remember the word Caterham, and I must have sounded a right idiot as I stumbled over the name. They smiled and nodded, understanding where I meant. I slouched into the corner and focused my eyes on one of those sepia tinted pictures – I remembered the ones I had seen on my first train journey years before.

The doubts suddenly came crowding in as the train pulled out. 'Have I done the right thing? No!' I thought to myself and my guts churned. From where I sat I could see the guard jumping in and out and waving his flag at each station. I more or less dozed off as the train rattled across the intersecting points. Through almost closed eyelids I glanced over to the couple and saw that they were looking at me – our eyes met and we grinned, embarrassed. When the guard yelled 'Whyteleafe' they got out and I was left alone with my doubts and tightening stomach muscles. The adrenalin was really flowing as the train sped out into the outer suburbs and hills of the North Downs. My mind was going up and down with excitement and fear like a bloody yo-yo. I lit yet another fag to calm myself and suddenly 'Caterham' was yelled and before you could say 'Jack Robinson' out I leapt and stood quivering on the platform, feeling very vulnerable. There were others climbing out and walking down the platform in front of me. 'Strange', I thought as I passed their carriage and noticed 'RESERVED' stickers on the windows, but I was certain they were heading for the same destination.

Outside the station stood a three-ton lorry and a corporal armed with an official looking clip board. He was busy checking off the group against the list he had, each one climbing up into the lorry as he was checked off. 'They must be conscripts', I said to myself, 'and here's me, a volunteer, having to make me own way!' I thought of hitching a lift and then thought 'Bugger it – I'll stay independent a bit longer!'

I looked around me and saw a hill. I hadn't a clue where to go next, and the lorry hadn't moved, probably waiting for another group. There were some shops but I didn't feel like asking in them. I felt that the barracks would be at the top of the hill so I started to walk up it. I hadn't got far when I saw a wizen-faced old man coming in the opposite direction. He had on a slouched old trilby pulled very low over his forehead. Below his dirty rain coat, his trouser bottoms were clasped by bicycle clips. He was riding an old black Phillips roadster in a scooter fashion – one foot on the road and the other on the pedal. What I noticed in particular was the nice shiny bell on the handlebar – it glinted and twinkled as he rode down on his brakes. I stepped out in the road.

'Excuse me, mister, d'you know where Caterham Depot is?' He peered at me, his watery blue eyes sizing me up – his face revealing more lines in close-up than any teacher had given me for punishment.

'Look, son', he said, 'you climb this 'ere 'ill to the top – that's where you'll find the barricks.' He smiled – 'an' don't go inter the wrong entrance – you might find it 'ard ter get out!' He cackled at this and resumed scooting his bike down the hill before I could question him further. I couldn't understand what the joke was, but at least he wasn't lost! So I plodded up the hill, turning to look back over my shoulder as I got towards the top and being rewarded by a lovely view of the surrounding countryside. The view made the long plod up that hill a lot easier. Ahead I could see a high wall. 'This must be it', I thought and walked towards the gate. Just before I got to the gate I read a sign on the gatepost and suddenly realised what the old boy's joke was about. It was a bloody lunatic asylum!! 'Saucy ol' sod', I muttered, as I beat a confused and hasty retreat and walked further along to the next gateway.

The gates of the depot were open and I stood out of sight of the sentry for a while before I could bring myself to go in. ''Scuse me mate, is this the Caterham Guard's Depot?' No reply. I repeated this two or three times, each time louder – I even tried coughing. I must have looked a real twerp standing there one foot inside and one outside the entrance gate holding my small brown attache case, yelling at the top of my voice to a sentry who didn't move a muscle. Suddenly a huge corporal came charging out of the guardhouse close by.

'What's goin' on 'ere? Wot d'you want?', he demanded. 'You mustn't talk to a sentry on duty.'

'Who else am I to talk to?', I replied, beginning to lose my cool. 'Look, mate, there's no name, no sign, no number and I'm supposed to report 'ere!'

'Show me your papers then.' The creases in his trousers had the same knife edge as his voice had. He shooed me into the guardhouse – I had crossed the threshold at last! – and scrutinised my papers while I had a good 'butchers' around the room: some bunks and a couple of cells – just like the ones in the cowboy films – even rifles in racks on the walls. The place reeked of disinfectant, the floors were scrubbed and there were a couple of squaddies sitting on bunks. I stared at them fascinated – their short hair was little more than stubble, just like the wheatfields after harvest. They looked lean, hard and healthy in their grey denims. I wondered what you had to do to get into those cells. By now the corporal was on the blower. 'Yes, recruit McCarthy', I could hear, 'Yes sir' and the 'ting' of a phone being replaced followed by the clumping of boots.

'Here you are', he said, handing me back my papers. 'You'll have to hang about – would you like a mug of tea?'

My spirits rose. 'Yes please, mate. Er – corporal.'

That was one of the two nicest moments I could recall at Caterham. The other was leaving the place.

Note

1. *Boysie* (Braunton, Devon: Merlin, 1986) p. 3.

2

All the King's Men

From the guardhouse I was escorted by a guardsman dressed in denim to the reception block. On the way my eyeballs were doing overtime – I could see the perimeter wall of the depot stretching away into the distance. On the large tarmac parade ground troops were busy square bashing, drilled by a sergeant wielding a pace stick; he was screaming out commands and abuse while he was pacing, picking out named individuals for particular insults if they made mistakes. Around the parade ground were long sheds open on one side, with mirrors on some of their walls and I wondered what they could be for. I thought I'd better get a bit of early practice in by trying to keep in step with my escort, but I made a bad job of it as I was so busy looking at other things. Coming to the corner of a block of buildings my escort stopped suddenly and turned and I only just avoided running into him.

'This is it mate, go up to the barrack room on the first floor and wait there.'

'Thanks mate', I muttered, and he nodded and grinned as he turned away. Climbing a flight of stone stairs I reached the first floor and turned into a long ward-like room with several bunks or cot beds. I plonked myself down on one, laid my case beside me and looked round the high ceilinged room. The floor was highly polished and the walls between the windows and at either end held plaques recalling battle honours from years ago, with regimental colours above them. I was all alone so I chanced a fag to try to calm my nervousness. Soon I heard footsteps and a young chap, portly for his age, came in. 'Hello', he said 'I'm Duggie.'

'Pleased to meet you Duggie, I'm Boysie', I replied, glad to have company.

'This must be the reception place', said Duggie, as he opened his case on the bed next to mine. 'Want a bit of chocolate, Boysie?' I could see dozens of bars of the stuff inside his case.

'Blimey! 'Ow did yer manage ter get 'old of all that chocolate – bin savin' it up?'

'No – a friend of a friend – you know what I mean,' replied Duggie grinning, and soon we were chatting and munching like old friends. He looked prosperous; he had on a good quality grey suit that had never seen the likes of shops such as Nobby Berg's or the 50/- Tailors. He said his father was in the men's outfitting trade and had a small shop on Tottenham Court Road.

'Hey, Duggie – it ain't Hornes is it?' I queried. He didn't say yes or no to that, leaving my imagination to provide the answer.

Soon several more recruits arrived and the noise in the room got louder and louder. We introduced ourselves in the offhand way one does – there must have been twenty of us altogether, all of us volunteers and belonging to all five foot guards regiments. The Cockney accents of the Londoners amongst us immediately bound us together in friendship. Funny how you cling to anything familiar when in a strange situation.

Suddenly a sergeant marched into the room and an immediate silence descended – no one felt inclined to call attention to himself right then. He told us that we would be sleeping there that night and that early next morning we were to line up outside. He disappeared and the chat resumed, to be broken later by the sound of a bugle in the distance. None of us knew what it was for, then someone suggested that it might mean lights out so, stripping off to our underpants, we bedded down for the night, making do with what we had. It was a long time before we dropped off: strange noises, hard beds, new events and more than a little apprehension kept our minds active. Eventually all fell silent except for the snores of a couple of the lads.

Next morning a bugle blown outside the windows woke us up. Very soon the bugle call was repeated some distance away, quickly followed by a repeat performance from yet another place. Suddenly a rush and clatter of hobnailed boots and a raucous voice shattered the peace of the room. 'Get outa bed you 'orrible lot, cum on, get outa yer wankin' pits!' We shot out of our beds more in fright than anything else and stood there staring at this apparition of authority. 'I want you downstairs in twenty minutes washed and shaved. NOW GET A MOVE ON' yelled the corporal and we winced as he turned and marched out of sight.

To our disgust there were not enough washing facilities to go round and we had to queue for everything. We took it out on each other, the townies among us yelling at the fellows from the sticks who had almost immediately been labelled swede-bashers. 'Get out of the trough and let another pig in!' A quick soapy wet shave and a wipe round with a wet hand and we charged down the stone stairs and lined up outside more dead than alive. Dawn was just breaking as a sergeant with a clip board addressed us.

'Right, pay attention. When I call your name out get into your respective group or squad. Brown.'

A voice just behind me answered: 'Yes, sarge.'

'Grenadiers. Collins – Coldstreams.' And so on. Suddenly I heard my name: 'McCarthy.'

'Sir', I replied.

'Irish Guards.'

I was appalled. I stepped forward. 'Excuse me sarge, I joined the Grenadiers, not the Irish Guards.'

A snigger came from the lads around, quickly silenced by a glare from the formidable character addressing us. He checked through the papers on his clip board as I held my breath. He looked up and stared at me; 'So you did, lad – so you did – Grenadiers it is.'

Heaving a sigh of relief I scuttled over to the group before he could change his mind. Soon we were lined up in our regiments. I noticed that there were eight of us in the Grenadiers – more than in any other regiment. 'More of us bein' killed I expect', I thought morbidly – probably with good reason!

'After you've noshed in the canteen go back to yer barrack room and collect yer gear, you'll be escorted from there to your new regimental lines. Grenadiers will stay put. You'll all be kitted out afterwards, OK?' And off he marched before any of us could answer. Nosh consisted of porridge, powdered egg and a mug of tea that I swear had so much bromide in you could stand a teaspoon up in it!

'What size boots are yer, lad?', says the quartermaster.

'Nine' and a pair of hobnailed boots are slammed on the counter and you move on.

'Chest size?'

'40' And a tunic lands in your arms.

'Cop 'old of this.' The peaked cap rammed on my head falls over my ears. A second one is a bit better. I'm also issued with a forage cap with a plastic cap badge.

''Ere mate, 'ow abaht a brass grenade for me peaked 'at then – the regimental one!'

'What you got there?' says the bloke behind the counter, looking at the cap, and, seeing that there is no badge there shoves a brass grenade badge towards me. ''Ere y'are then.'

'Ta mate' and I go off satisfied.

Loaded with what seemed everything but the kitchen sink we staggered back to the barrack room to sort ourselves out. Jack Whitehouse, a strapping lad of 6ft 8ins from the Black Country, had no trousers. His long legs (long enough to qualify for the Bluebell Girls but maybe too hairy) stuck out way beyond any pair they had in stock. While we were struggling to sew the red and white flashes bearing the regiment's name on to the tunic sleeves the curses came thick and fast as our clumsy fingers were stabbed by the sharp pointed needles and the thread persisted in knotting itself. We discussed ways to slit the peaks of the caps and refix them so that they came down over our eyes, which was considered 'flash'. One bloke (a bit of a know all) told us it was meant to keep your head up as that was the only way you could see where you were going when the peak was worn in that fashion.

'You reckon?'

'Yeah.'

The barrack room began to take on a friendly, familiar atmosphere, almost a haven in the confusion, as we began to get to know one another. It wasn't long before we were on the move again though. Late that evening we were told to collect our gear and get over to the second floor in Wellington Block. It was all we could do to carry the stuff and climb the stone stairs. Loaded up with as much as I could carry I started to climb. The iron bannisters on my right were low and we were in danger of tipping over, top heavy as we were with the gear on our shoulders. We were coming up the stairs, keeping well over to the right as other squaddies came down, when suddenly I found myself being pushed almost over the bannister by someone yelling 'Move over you shit bag.' I saw red and promptly slung everything I was carrying on top of him.

'No one speaks to me like that, you bastard', I shouted, 'cop that' – and pushed his head hard against the wall, my outstretched hand over his face. He was covered with bedclothes and my army greatcoat and sitting on the stairs wondering what had happened. Spluttering with shock and rage he got back to his feet. 'Do you realise who I am?' he demanded pointing to two stripes on his arm.

'I don't care who the f...... 'ell you are', I retorted.

'I'm a corporal, you stoopid git. What's yer name?' I told him.

'You're on a charge, McCarthy. You'll be in front of the CO [the Commanding Officer] in the morning!' and stormed off, not seeing the V sign I gave him as I gathered up my gear. There was silence as I plodded back over to get some more clobber. 'Bloody 'ell', I thought. 'What a start, only bin in the 'Kate Carney' [Army] 24 hours and I'm already on a blinkin' charge!' Having completed the transfer without further incident, I chose a bunk near the far end close to the one belonging to the trained soldier who was there to look after us and show us the ropes. He was a Dunkirk veteran and seemed (and was) years older than us lads. We had moved in with the conscripts who had arrived over the past few days and our arrival made up a complete squad of twenty, all of us Grenadiers.

There was a sergeant, a corporal and a young officer in charge of the squad as well as the trained soldier. The sergeant was something of a hero figure to us. He held the George Medal, having won it as a police-man in the bombing of the London Docks, an attack I had watched in speechless fury from Archway Bridge.[1] He was a good looking bloke, dapper almost, with a moustache – he was also extremely fit. He had been a peacetime regular for years and had been recalled to the colours not long after his medal-winning exploits.

The tale of my fracas with the foul mouthed corporal soon spread through the barrack room and I found that I was already gaining a rep-utation among the squad. It didn't comfort me much the next morn-ing though, as I stood, hands clammy with nerves, as stiff as a board in front of the CO. I had been marched there at the double and lis-tened intently as the charge was read out, making sure I wasn't being accused of anything I hadn't done. 'Shut yer gob, till yer told ter speak' had been the explicit instructions of the trained soldier just be-fore I had left the barrack room.

'Look here McCarthy, assaulting an NCO on your first day – dear, dear man, this won't do. Have you anything to say?', asked the CO, more in sorrow than in anger.

I remembered the preliminary ritual and said 'Thank you sir for leave to speak' before telling him how I had been pushed aside and sworn at without reason. The captain listened as he had no doubt lis-tened so many times to the tale of whoever was in front of him. My two escorts stared ahead expressionless, their eyes hidden behind the slashed and repinned peaks of their caps. I wondered what they were thinking.

I was brought back to earth by the CO's tired refined voice. 'Seven days confined to barracks, fatigues and reporting to the guardroom.' I was marched out at the double at what seemed the speed of an express train, back to the sanctuary of the barrack room where the inmates were waiting to hear what had gone on.

The old soldier came over and said simply 'Well?'

'Seven days', I said glumly.

'Never mind, son', he said. 'You're never a guardsman till you've done a bit of poky.'

'Yeah – but I'm still only a bleedin' recruit', I retorted.

For the next thirteen weeks life was sheer hell. We spent much of the time wishing we had never been born as we rushed from polishing (we called it bullshitting) to square bashing and from bayonet practice to rifle drill. At times we didn't know whether we were at 'arsehole or breakfast time' as we crudely put it during this phase of training – one thing for sure, the finished product would be grade AOK, but we still had a long way to go. There seemed to be a different outfit for each ac-tivity and we got in each others' way in the rush to keep up and not be late. We lived in a haze of confusion, exhaustion and hunger and all our spare cash was spent on food in the NAAFI. When I had signed on I had made over 7/- a week to Mum which left me with 10/- one week and only 5/- the next. I was always short of cash to buy polish and extra food. The first week was unbelievable. I had the fatigues to do on top of everything else; I spent what little free time I had cleaning out the latrines, spud bashing and floor scrubbing.

Our first parade was a calamity. We could neither keep in step nor move our arms in unison; we seemed to have two left feet and two right arms. 'Cooper! Don't you know your right from your left yet? And try keepin' in step!', yells the sergeant. 'Raven! Stop laughing in the ranks' and he strides up to him: 'You snivellin' little git! Get a hold of yerself, man! Right. We will stay here all night if necessary to get it right.' The clatter of a dropped rifle shatters the silence – someone hisses 'Pick the bastard thing up or we'll be 'ere all bleedin night!' The punishment for the culprit was to hold the 9lb rifle above his head until told to take it down.

''Ere 'Arry, I reckon the sarge will die of old age before 'e knocks us lot into shape', I mutter out of the corner of my mouth.

A few mornings later we stood before a bag stuffed with straw suspended from a gibbet like structure and wondered what was going to happen next. We discovered that this was for bayonet practice and we queued in single file to have a bash. We were told to make a noise when charging but all I could think of at the time was what the bookies shouted at the race meetings. '6 to 4 the field' and 'Even-stevens.' I shouted this out as I charged the dummy and bayonetted it up to the hilt. The sergeant came over and asked if I was running a book as I was shouting the odds.

'Sorry, Sarge, it's all I could think of – mind you we could clean up on the number of blokes not gettin' it right, couldn't we?'

He grinned; 'Alright, get in line you 'orrible shower and try again.'

Some of the guys got their bayonet stuck in the sack and one shied off the idea, only for the corporal to cut his finger and smear some of his blood across the sack and beckon the bloke to take a lunge. We practised this until we got it right – it could mean life or death in battle.

Kit inspection was another nightmare, everyone busy hunting for replacements to make up for what had been lost or nicked. Small items such as spoons and mess tins were always missing. The ritual part was to remember the lines as well as your army number. If you had anything missing it was 'Away for repair, sir.' Every item of your kit had to be displayed together with your blankets, all arranged neatly on your bed. I was forever in trouble over my badly darned socks, a situation aggravated by occupying the bunk next to Johnny, a mate of mine who was married. Johnny's socks were always beautifully darned and I was frequently being shown them as an example of how they should be repaired. What the officer didn't know was that the crafty sod used to send them home to be darned by his missus. I just couldn't win that one. I got so fed up having to compete with Johnny's wife's darning skills that when the opportunity arose I moved to the other side of the room, where my lack of darning skills didn't show up so badly.

The intensive training and square bashing took its toll on most of us in one way or another. My left heel literally turned red, black and blue, and it was so painful that I couldn't walk properly; friction between my foot and my boot had rubbed large areas of my heel and ankle raw. One evening at the 'Stand by yer beds' call from the corporal who took names for the next morning's sick parade to see the MO, I gave my name in. I limped wincing into the medical inspection hut and thankfully took off my boot at the orderly's request. When my turn came I hobbled into the MO's room, boot in hand. The doctor was old, judging by the grey hair on his head. He had lots of red patches on his tunic, I remember, and when he eventually finished shuffling the papers on his desk he looked up and fixed me with an ice cold gaze from a pair of fishy eyes.

'What's wrong with you?'

'It's my heel, sir – it's bruised and very painful. I can hardly get my boot on or walk.' He took a cursory look at my heel, without moving from his chair.

'Stop skiving and wasting my time', he barked, as he resumed shuffling papers. I was flabbergasted and was quickly ushered out of the room before I could speak, which maybe was just as well – the names I called him under my breath left him parentless. No treatment, not even ointment, and my heel was a mess and weeping.

'Bugger this for a lark!', I thought, as I struggled to pull on my grey coarse woollen sock and then, worse still, my boot. I hobbled as best as I could through the next parade. It was the trained soldier who eventually came to the rescue. On his advice I started soaking my feet in salt water, scrounged from a girl in the NAAFI. I eventually nursed my heel and ankle back to normal, but it took nearly three weeks.

The pressure was unrelenting as we struggled to learn the skills and reach the standards required. There were times when some blokes talked about climbing over the wall, but none of us was ever sure which was the right wall to climb. It was very high and if they got it wrong they would land in the lunatic asylum's yard, going from one mad house to another.

At one point we were moved out of the chilly high ceilinged barrack room in the old Wellington Block to some wooden huts which were much warmer and cosier. As we moved out, new recruits moved in – a guardsman factory. The whole place was geared to training young men to a high degree of fitness and battle readiness in the minimum of time, for the second front had begun and the war was at a critical stage. Much of the pressure stemmed from fear of not making the grade and being transferred to another regiment. This had happened to one or two in the block and none of us fancied it happening to us. The number of times I was called a millstone round the squad's neck was amazing. I was inclined to take it personally at first, but then I listened and learned that practically everyone else in the squad was also a millstone, so I stopped worrying.

Another frequently heard sentiment was 'You broke yer muvver's 'eart now we'll break yours.' This was the favourite saying of Company Sergeant Major Scaly, a small man by Guards' standards who made up in the quality and quantity of his voice what he lacked in stature. The first time I heard this voice and saw the size of its owner I couldn't believe it. 'Not another bleedin' Emma Cross', I thought. Emma had been a tiny neighbour of ours in the Bunk who had loads of kids and a very aggressive manner. Her voice could be heard giving her poor husband verbal GBH half way down the street when she really got going. I never saw the perfectly turned out CSM Scaly round the camp without being reminded of her.

As time passed, so the characters of the squad emerged, the know alls and the wheeler dealers, the comics and those with problems, the cocky ones and the nervous. We were beginning to develop into a fighting unit and soon realised how much we depended on each other's support. There were six of us from London in the squad and we soon palled up. The oldest of this sextet was Harry, who was twenty-eight and hailed from Forest Gate. He told us he was a company director – he certainly had the charm for the job, especially where the girls were concerned. A particular mate of mine was Johnny, who was married. Another of the gang had been a racing cyclist at the famous Herne Hill track where the six-day bike-races used to be held. Leslie's cycling had developed his leg muscles until his legs were like tree trunks – he was fitter and stronger than most of us in the beginning, but we soon caught up.

Very different was Cliff, a Salvation Army bloke from the Baker's Arms in the East End. He had the huge frame of a heavyweight boxer and was engaged to a girl also in the Sally Army who had lost a leg in the Blitz.

Duggie, suave, polished and much more the city gent than us Cockney sparrows, was one of us none the less. His baby face belied a clever brain and he never let his slightly paunchy body prevent his keeping up with the squad on exercises and other physically demanding activities. He exuded a quiet confidence which made you feel you could invest your money (not that we ever had any) in him without any qualms.

The six of us stuck together through thick and thin. I also struck up a close friendship with Jack Whitehouse, although we were as different as chalk from cheese. He was huge and powerful, a farm lad from Staffordshire whereas I was the smallest in the squad and on the skinny side, at little over 9 stone. A regular townie.

Several of the squad were over 6ft 6ins tall and big with it, their feet sticking out from beneath the blankets as the beds were on the small size. In the mornings, on a trip to the bogs, I would tickle their feet there and back, dodging a barrage of boots slung in retaliation.

Visits to the camp dentist were the bane of our already miserable lives. My teeth were in bad condition and after one particularly painful session, in which the sod took out my top front teeth with only the minimum of painkiller, I staggered out with a very sore mouth and swollen face. I stopped outside the door and lit a fag to calm my nerves. I had just taken the first gasp when I spotted an officer cycling towards me. I saluted him and when he saw me he yelled 'Take that bloody cigarette out of your mouth.' I had forgotten all about the fag, because I couldn't feel it in my numbed lips.

I grabbed it and hid it in my left hand, glancing over just in time to see the officer lose control of the bike. It hit the kerb, shooting him arse over head into the bushes as I took to my heels and ran behind the huts.

An hour later we were in battledress, square bashing again, my face and rifle butt caked in blood from my bleeding mouth. I didn't notice it too much – I was too busy fighting down surges of laughter and keeping my face straight at the memory of that officer in a heap in the bushes.

I felt the loss of my teeth badly and shrank into my shell. It didn't help that a week or so later there was to be a dance in the depot gym. The organisers needed a volunteer to check the tickets at the door and the sergeant volunteered me. 'OK, McCarthy, you can stand at the door and check the tickets and see no gatecrashers get in.' Some ATS and local ladies had been invited and I was unhappy at the idea of them seeing me in my gummy state. 'But sarge, I can't, not looking like this', I lisped.

'That's an order.' His tone didn't invite further argument. I was furious. 'When is this dance?', I asked.

'Week Saturday.'

The gang were sympathetic.

'Never mind Boysie, someone's got ter be bouncer. You can scare the 'ell outa them wiv yer fangs.' My misery lasted until two days before the dance, when I was summoned back to the dentist. I went in, vowing that the sod wasn't going to take out any more of my teeth. To my joy he snapped in a bridge with two lovely shiny new front teeth. I joked with the dentist about no longer being able to scare the gate-crashers with my fangs. He laughed, sensing my relief and joy at looking OK again and said that they considered it a matter of urgency to cover gaps in the front teeth as quickly as possible. So they were human after all! I ran back to the barrack room like a greyhound after a hare and standing in the middle of the room treated them all to a huge toothy grin.

'Hey, spiv – let's 'ave a butchers at yer pearlies.'

I repeated the biggest grin I could manage and a great howl of cheering went up. I was slapped on the back so hard they nearly knocked my new choppers out of my mouth.

'Well done my ol' son.'

'Good ol' spiv.'

'We knew you'd make it mate.'

At that point the sergeant walked in, wondering what all the commotion and whistling was about.

'Wot's this? 'Oo's that good lookin' fella there?', he demanded, grinning at my obvious delight. What a difference two little teeth had made to my life!

'Sarge, we won't stand no chance with the fluff nah that Boysie's got 'is teef in. You can't put 'im on the door nah – 'e'll pinch all the birds before we can get a look in.'

Suddenly I had become quite pleased at the prospect of being ticket collector cum bouncer; my Bunk trained mind, geared to turning any situation to my benefit, had soon worked out the possibilities, and I wasn't about to give up the job without a fight.

'Cam on sarge, what's the difference between last week and now, apart from my new look, that is?'

The sergeant looked at me thoughtfully and after a moment: 'OK lad, the job's yours still', amid groans and mock protests from the rest of the lads.

Not only did I have a ball that night with the ladies, having chatted up the tastiest of them as I took their tickets – I also got in for nothing! Even in khaki the girls managed to look terrific. The affairs of that evening were strictly one night stands as we were all more or less confined to barracks for the duration of our initial training – no chance of a more permanent arrangement. I soon found a girl to dance with who worked for the NAAFI on camp. 'Not bad', I thought. 'Not too far to walk her home. Might be good for an extra cuppa and wad.' She was very pretty with blue eyes, blonde hair and a well developed sense of humour. She was called Dorothy and came from Norwich.

I was reasonably happy with my new look, thanks to my new teeth, and planned to have a photograph taken to send to Mum and Dad. I was wondering how to go about it as I walked towards the NAAFI a couple of days later but while indulging in a scrounged cuppa and a rock cake (a particularly apt name in this case), I broke my precious new teeth while biting into the latter. I was horrified and made a speedy exit, handkerchief to mouth, shooting straight round to the dentist. Rapid repairs were needed if I was to keep up my new image. I didn't want to be out of circulation as far as my love life was concerned. Luckily the dentist was able to fix the teeth straight away — much to my relief.

Towards the end of our stay a rumour went round that we were being moved in about a week's time — no one knew where but the rumour persisted and we were excited at the prospect.

One morning the squad was lined up to have its photograph taken. I had overdone the straightening of the peak on my cap and had to tip my head back to see where I was going. We assumed that we must have all passed muster and we were mightily relieved. Our joy was complete a day or so later when we were allowed outside the depot for an afternoon and evening in Caterham; our first free time outside for thirteen weeks! As we strolled down the hill into the village our hobnailed boots rang on the tarmac of the road and our voices were loud with the sheer bliss of pressure removed and the prospect of free time. We couldn't believe this was happening as we made our way towards doing the things we had talked about — pubs, girls and photos taken for mums and wives. Johnny and I decide to have our photos taken at a local photographers and while he posed I suggested that the photographer charged double to cover the damage to his camera. Johnny retaliated by suggesting that I needed a numbered board across my chest.

By opening time our tongues were hanging out, some of the lads were scoffing fish and chips and we were waiting outside our chosen pub when Harry strolled by with a good looking bird on his arm. Harry did tend to fancy himself a bit: he was always rather secretive, especially when it came to whether he was married or not — to this day I'm not sure.

'Wotcha 'Arry', I called as they strolled by, he looking a bit self conscious. ''Oos lookin' after the kids then?'

Harry coloured up and glared at me, the girl looked at him quizzically and Harry laughed it off as they turned the corner.

As we stood there shivering in the cold wind the pub doors opened and we all poured in. Never had a pint tasted so good. As I sat there with the froth still on my upper lip Harry walked in, minus the bird. I wondered what had happened. 'Allo, 'Arry, on yer Jack?'

'Yeah, no thanks to you', growled Harry as he dipped into his pint. After a few silent moments, the beer began to exercise its mellowing effect and he grinned at me over the top of his glass.

'Do me a favour, Boysie – I'm the company director and I'm single, savvy?' he said, as he polished the brass grenade on his cap with his tunic sleeve.

'Yeah, sure 'Arry, you can count on me mate. Sorry abaht the bird just nah', I replied. 'It'll cost yer a pint mind', I added, 'if that's the way you want ter play it, me ol' china! By the way, if we're pairin' off I'll always 'ave the ugly one.'

Harry looked at me puzzled, but I was busy with my nose in the beer again.

'Naturally', he said after a short delay, 'naturally.'

We had a great time that evening – the pub had a piano and soon 'Roll out the barrel' and other old favourites were being hammered out and sung at the tops of our voices.

During the evening a couple of little beauties came in and sat near-by. Neither of us wasted any time and soon we were chatting them up as hard as we could go. Harry was charming them with his suave manner (he could charm the birds off the trees). 'This is Boysie', he introduced me with a wave of his hand. They really were a couple of corkers: bright red lipstick on full shapely lips and more curves than a Yankee baseball pitcher.

'Hy'a honey', I drawled, trying to act suave too and homing in on the one with eye lashes literally inches long and a face like Bette Davis.

Harry's voice hissed in my ear: 'That one's mine.'

'Sorry mate, all's fair in love and war.'

Harry glared at me before the diplomatic approach reasserted itself as he turned again to the girls. 'Time for a drink, ladies', he said, getting up.

'No, we'll get these, lads', one of the girls replied firmly, pushing Harry back into his seat and heading for the bar, leaving us astounded.

'Incredible. I don't believe it', Harry said eventually. A minute later we were wading into two more pints bought for us by the two beauties.

I later managed to get my bird behind the blackout curtain near the door and we started to kiss and cuddle in the gap between the pub door and the thick curtain, but we gave it up as a bad job after being squashed several times by the door as people pushed it to get in. That evening was magic: booze flowed from all quarters and we didn't pay for any of it.

By the time we were due to return to barracks most of us were pissed out of our minds as we staggered back up the hill. 'I 'ope that photographic bugger sends me photos 'ome', I muttered to Jack, who was next to me at the time.

'That's my boy, Spiv', laughed Jack, my Black Country mate, as he tripped over his size 12 boots and fell on his knees. The rest of the journey was completed with the pair of us holding each other up – a lopsided arrangement as he was a good eight inches taller than me and over four stone heavier. As we reached the top of the hill and the barrack gates so the horseplay and singing gave way to the straightening of uniforms and caps and concentrated attempts to stay upright. It was back to business again once inside. That night the conversation among those of us who stayed conscious was mainly about the birds that got away, the nearly made its. The quiet ones I reckoned must have made it and were keeping it to themselves. There were several missing when we got back to the hut.

Our squad had its passing out parade the next morning; from that time on we were officially guardsmen and no longer recruits. We lined up outside the huts with fixed bayonets led by our young officer, the sergeant and the corporal. We had been transformed from a motley crew of conscripts and volunteers whose first attempts at marching had created chaos to a tall walking, highly disciplined crew as tough as old boots. The machine had spat us out and our next destination was a place called Windsor.

Note

1. *Boysie*, p.155.

3

Windsor

'All right, you chaps. Form up into threes', shouted a young officer with a plummy accent as we disembarked from the train onto the platform. So this was Windsor – I had heard often enough about it, but I'd never been there.

I hid myself in the middle of the squad and we marched off behind the officer and an NCO. Soon I could see the castle surrounded by its high wall. Nearer were the bow-fronted shop fronts and in front of them groups of people standing and staring at us as we marched by, heads high, arms swinging and the studs of our boots ringing in unison against the cobbles of the hill. Quite a contrast to the chaos of our earlier attempts as raw recruits a few months before.

'It's the Guards', I heard a couple of old dears say as we marched past, and I felt a surge of pride at being a part of them. We passed Queen Victoria's statue, but that feature was less interesting to us than the cafe across the road from the barrack entrance. I filed that bit of intelligence away for future reference.

'Keep in step': the order was barked out by the NCO as we rounded the corner and swung through Sheet Street into Victoria Barracks. We turned into the narrow entrance to find that the guard had turned out to welcome us. The butts of the rifles were slapped in unison as arms were presented and it was 'eyes left' as we turned before being dismissed outside a large gaunt brick building. On reaching our new sleeping quarters there was a scramble for the bunks in the best spots. I got one opposite the stove and away from Johnny and his beautifully darned socks. We all collapsed on our beds and were just relaxing when a corporal told us to be in the adjoining hall in fifteen minutes, where the Regimental Sergeant Major wanted to say a few words to us. Some were inclined to think that we were going to be sent abroad, others had more flippant suggestions. 'Harry's got a girl in the family way', one wag claimed.

'Nah – I only use executive type quality rubber goods', replied Harry coolly.

Before any more could be said a new voice was heard ...

'Blimey more smoke in 'ere than Battersea Power Station!' A large moustached Company Sergeant Major, who had come in almost unnoticed, was busy sizing us up. 'Cigarettes out, gents!', he ordered and we jumped to obey. 'Git yerselves in the 'all next door nah' and out we scuttled, sensing that to upset this giant would not be the most rewarding of experiences.

At the far end of the hall was yet another wax-moustached giant, this one with a haircut so short that he looked almost bald – like a skinhead needing a shave. He had enormous shoulders and boots. Sewn on his sleeve was an outsize badge bearing a coat of arms. He stood there motionless as we scrambled into our seats, trying not to be last and call attention to ourselves. He had a furrowed brow and screwed up his eyes as he stood there, hands clasped in front of him.

'Close the door, you lad at the back.' This done he embarked on his talk – which turned out to be on the one subject we hadn't even thought of. 'I want to warn you newcomers abaht some men who frequent pubs – I'll call 'em "twisters".'

We looked at each other disbelievingly and some of us fought surges of laughter. 'Does he mean poofs, queers, Nancy boys?', we enquired of each other, and one brave soul asked the question out loud.

'No, I mean "twisters"', replied the RSM stonily. 'If they buy you a drink don't get involved', he continued, against a background of laughter, ribald comments and camp gestures. So this was the big talk – no dispatching abroad, no drama, just 'Watch out for Nancy boys!' The consensus of opinion was 'stupid old sod', but at least it gave us a good laugh.

Some of us in our innocence thought that our intensive training at Caterham was the end of it. How wrong we were! We had just learned the basics there, it seemed, and now we were to learn how to endure exhaustion and stress and still perform as a crack fighting unit. There was no let up in pressure, we just gradually became more skilled and able to meet the demands made on us.

In spite of the unrelenting pressure and demanding routine we soon settled into the new way of life. The original twenty of our squad had been added to and now we were a platoon – thirty-six of us. The regional loyalties remained strong and we Cockneys stuck together as did other cliques, particularly those from the north country and the south west. Compared with Caterham, life at Windsor wasn't bad at all. The highlight of the day was around 7p.m. when you could get a free cuppa and a wad from the canteen. Sometimes it was a delicious sausage roll or a hot pie and it made a lovely supper. If you looked lively you could even scrounge seconds.

Forced marches of up to forty miles carrying full packs were a feature of our training at Windsor. We were pushed to our limits on these marches and after each one we were only too glad to lie flat on our backs with our feet in the air for the platoon officer to inspect them for blisters. On one particularly warm and humid day we were on such a march and blokes were flaking out left, right and centre. I remember one poor sod collapsing in the road only 100 yards from the barrack gates, but we were too far gone to help, loaded as we were with all our heavy gear. We knew an orderly would be sent out so didn't think anything of it as we stepped over his body, but two old ladies witnessed the incident, saw us carry on ignoring him and took matters into their own hands. They chased us into the barracks and laid about the nearest officers with their umbrellas, telling the NCOs and the officer exactly what they thought of him while they clobbered the pair of them. I was too far away to hear exactly what was being said – but it was obvious they meant business.

On another forced march in and around Windsor Great Park I dropped out for a breather: my legs were like jelly and wouldn't do as they were told any longer. I knew the others would be stopping for rifle and machine gun practice and planned to catch them up then.

As I walked along a long road in the park I spotted an army lorry approaching and promptly thumbed a lift. As I looked hard at the driver I realised, with a jolt, that it was Princess Elizabeth. Needless to say she turned off without stopping and disappeared from view. I spent the rest of the march thinking what a pity it was she didn't give me a lift. We could have chatted about Buckingham Palace being bombed and my mate, Curly, being badly injured while on guard duty outside. 'My God', I thought, 'think of the consequences, being dropped off at the platoon by HRH.' 'One of yours, I believe'. Never mind. Eventually I caught up with the rest of the group, to be met by the sergeant in charge.

'What happened to you, McCarthy?'

'Sorry sarge – call of nature – rough night last night.'

'Well don't make a 'abit of it.'

'No, sarge.'

'Get on that bren gun and see if you can 'it that target.'

'Yes Sarge' and I scuttled over to the bren gun, fell flat on my face, aimed and fired. When the score came back I had hit right across the centre of the target five times. I was dead chuffed.

Target practice completed we had to get back to Victoria Barracks, at first at a brisk pace then at the double, passing a group of squaddies at Combermere Barracks, the Household Cavalry's base at Windsor. During wartime their horses were replaced by tanks (to withstand machine gun bullets better, no doubt). As we passed there were plenty of taunts, but we'd been ordered to keep quiet so we couldn't retaliate.

My legs were turning to jelly again under the weight of my equipment plus the tripod of a bren gun which had been passed back by someone up front on the point of collapse. I protested 'Sorry mate, I can barely carry me own bundock (rifle)', and passed it on down the ranks. God help the blokes in the back row – they'd no one to pass the unwanted stuff to. Several lads had passed out and now I was carrying two rifles. At last we were out of the Great Park and the barrack gates came into view. I was mightily relieved when we slowed to a walking pace.

A regular event at Windsor was the Saturday five-mile battalion run around the Great Park. Anyone who got back to base before the third bugle call got a thirty-six-hour pass. At the third blast a rope was stretched across the track and all those inside had their names taken and got the passes. Try as we might we never got in on time – there were 400 men running and many were club or professional runners – but Harry, Johnny and I hit on a solution. While on our circuits we passed crowds watching football matches. I realised that if we joined the crowd and waited for the next lap we could join the front runners. We were careful not to get in too early – they weren't stupid – and we timed it to get in between the second and third bugle calls. The plan worked and we got our passes.

Mounting guard at the castle was part of our life at Windsor. We were led out by a fife and drum band, which I loved. At night the sentries wore plimsolls and carried tommy-guns so as not to wake up the nearby residents. We always wore khaki – the red tunics and bearskins had been put away for the duration. There had been a scare about German parachutists dropping in and everyone was on the alert – I remember being on guard one morning when a slim bloke came by pushing a wheel barrow full of garden stuff and I was about to challenge him when I recognised him as King George. I saluted hurriedly as he drew level and he looked up, smiled briefly and wished me 'Good morning, sentry.'

One lad came in fuming one evening from duty at the main gate of the castle. Some American armed with a large camera had been making a nuisance of himself, asking him to look one way then another, pushing his girl friend right up against him and asking him to smile. Finally he had got so fed up that he hissed 'Piss off' out of the corner of his mouth. The bloke had such a shock he nearly dropped his camera and the pair scarpered quickly, amazed at the talking 'chocolate' soldier!

There were other tales, too. One sentry, on being accosted by a drunk and hugged so violently that his peaked cap was knocked to the floor, took a quick look round, saw no one was looking, put his rifle and bayonet down and calmly laid one on the drunk, knocking him out cold. He bundled him into his sentry box, picked up his rifle and cap and continued to pace up and down as if nothing had happened until a policeman walked by and was asked to help a 'gentlemen in distress'.

We were generally a pretty lighthearted bunch and as we became more practised in the skills we were learning we also grew in confidence. That confidence and lightheartedness were badly shaken in an incident which brought home to us the awful reality and waste of war.

One day we were marched to a firing range at Bisley. The exercises were now carried out with live ammo and we were going to have our first experience as targets. We were to take it in turns in groups of six, two standing, two kneeling and two sitting between two logs. We were being fired at by two marksmen with bren guns.

'This is bloody barmy', grumbled 'Nosher' Willis, as we got in position.

''Ow do they know there won't be any richochets?', I wanted to know.

'They 'it the dirt bank behind yer, at least that's what they're supposed to do.'

'You don't sound too sure, do yer', I answered.

When we were ready the command to fire was given and the red tracer bullets came sailing towards us, closely followed by the real things which whined and sang past us before hitting the dirt bank behind us with dull thuds. I was mesmerised by the tracer bullets as I stood there. Suddenly the direction of one of the stream of bullets altered and they began hitting the ground in front of us. Before we could think of doing anything one of the lads sitting in the front of our group slumped over. Blood was spurting everywhere, spattering us with red blotches and specks. Still the bullets came, flying around us; one of them clipped my webbing pouch pocket.

'Bugger this', I shouted, and dived flat. One guy was waving a handkerchief to attract attention. I shouted: 'Don't get outside the logs or it'll be yer lot!'

Eventually someone spotted that something was wrong – we were flat on our faces, waving our hands and shouting and at last the firing stopped. We rushed to poor Lenny, but he was past help – the bullet had smashed through his throat and he was dead. We stood aside trying to recover by lighting up fags while others tended to Lenny. A pool of blood spread over the ground in front of the logs and began to seep into the soil. We stood round him, covered in his blood and shocked to the core. Blokes came running over and pulled us away, and someone started being sick and I pulled at my fag with violently shaking hands. The site of the accident was being smothered in sand while an officer came over and took command. I turned round to see Harry standing next to me, ashen faced.

'I don't fancy goin' in there again', he said in a shaky voice.

'Bollocks to that', I answered. 'What the f...... 'ell went wrong over there?', I demanded of the gun crew who had come running over.

'Seems one was wrongly sited and fired too low, hitting the ground in front of yer', said one of them shakily.

'I'm wiv' yer on this one, Boysie', said Harry, 'I'm not fuckin' well goin' in there again to 'ave me 'ead blown off.'

At that moment the officer turned to us. 'Right, the same men back in again and add another to make up the number.'

No one moved, so a corporal came over.

'Look, yer've got ter get used to bein' under gun fire – you 'eard the officer.'

'Are you making up the vacancy, corp?' I asked, still shaking with shock.

'Don't be saucy, son', he growled.

We were edging slowly forward along the grass verge towards the site when a sergeant came over to report that the other bren had jammed and that the session would have to be cancelled. We heaved a huge sigh of relief and moved away, trying to be inconspicuous. The meat waggon arrived for Lenny's body and it was carted away. A few days later some of the lads travelled up to Luton for the military funeral. An inquest was held, but we never heard the result. Lenny was just another casualty as far as the powers that be were concerned.

A couple of weeks later we all piled into trains and were taken to Minehead, a small seaside town on the Somerset coast, where we were put up in a couple of vacant boarding houses opposite the hospital. We were there for a toughening up campaign – as if we needed it. There must have been more than 100 of us in this nice old resort, with its pubs and cinema, but we were there for the miles of rough Exmoor terrain which loomed up on the western edge of the town.

I nearly killed Harry up there when we were storming a deserted farmhouse. He was in an advance party moving forward in a smoke screen with crossfire coming from the right flank. We were about 200 yards behind, firing a mix of smoke and high explosive mortar bombs. I dropped one right next to Harry; luckily it was a smoke bomb. If it had been live he would have been in pieces all over the heather.

We moved forward just after that barrage and Harry met me as I scrambled down next to him. All his charm had disappeared and he yelled a string of unprintable obscenities at me – his good-looking face contorted in fury and covered in mud, heather and smoke. He was cut short and we both dived for cover as some nut started firing just above our heads.

'Get forward you silly sod', yelled a corporal nearby – 'You don't want ter kill yer own men now do yer.'

'No corp', the guy behind us replied innocently.

Harry growled 'You stupid pratt!' at him before we moved off to find better cover.

It was strange up there on top of the hills. A Spitfire or Hurricane would fly by through the valleys as we were resting, considerably lower than us, the pilot waving to us as we waved back. These intensive training exercises were killers – on one we climbed Porlock Hill in full battle gear, up a road with a gradient of 1 in 3 in places that went on for ever. Two girls sat on a bench watching us, solemnly licking ice cream cones as we sweated and puffed our way up the hill, lungs bursting and legs aching under the strain – that didn't help.

On one of the night exercises we climbed Dunkery Beacon, and established a temporary camp there. It was an eerie experience. The night was clear and the full moon gave enough light to show up the bodies of the sheep that had been hit in crossfire earlier that day. The empty spaces and the silence around us gave me the willies – I wasn't used to this kind of quietness and emptiness.

Once the exercises had finished we returned to Windsor and the castle. We marched through Slough station and down the High Street towards Windsor and I gazed at the distinctive chapel of Eton School and the green velvet of the playing fields. We marched over the bridge that crosses the Thames and I noticed the iron railway bridge to my right, in a single arc over the river. I would get a much closer view of it a couple of days later.

One evening later that week we were formed up and marched to that bridge and given instructions. We were to crawl up and over the iron framework and down the other side, with the river below and trains rumbling backwards and forwards in the gloom below our feet. As we clung, loaded with gear, to the knobs of rivets in the bridge we could see the passengers in the trains as they slowed into the station. Down below the river glistened like black ink. If we fell in there would be a mighty splash and I didn't fancy my chances, weighed down as I was: I couldn't swim very well. As I hung there I could hear every sound in the silence and gloom of the blackout; another train rumbled onto the bridge and the whole structure shuddered. At last we could see the other side clearly in the moonlight. I was mightily relieved to get back onto solid land – I have no head for heights.

Once everyone had been accounted for, we were ordered back to camp at the double. Back over the road bridge, up the hill, past the statue of Queen Victoria we pounded, puffing and blowing and into camp. Those of us who had any money made a beeline over to the cafe for a cuppa and beans on toast, or a sausage sandwich.

' 'Ere Boysie', Johnny mumbled through a mouthful. 'Fancy trying a dodgy thirty-six hour pass?'

'I dunno' I replied. I always seemed to be on jankers (fatigues) for doing something wrong or speaking out of turn and I didn't think I could stay away that long without being missed. 'Besides I ain't got enough for me fare.'

'Don't worry abaht that, I've got a plan fer gettin' round that. You just buy a ticket to the next station up the line from Windsor and the same coming back.'

'But 'ow d'yer manage roll call?' I still couldn't see how it was going to be possible to get away with it.

'I get a couple of mates to stand in for us'

'But what about the redcaps at Waterloo?' I persisted, worried about the military police. With a sigh of exasperation Johnny replied 'We won't go anywhere near Waterloo. I've got me route all worked out. Now are you coming or not?'

'OK. I trust yer', I said. 'We'll slip out of camp Saturday afternoon if there's nothin' going on.'

'Sports day is on', volunteered Johnny, who'd done his homework.

'OK then, I'll give it a try.'

True to his word Johnny arranged with a couple of mates to cover for us and on the Saturday afternoon we sauntered off on our dodgy thirty-six hour leave without so much as a pass between us. We bought two return tickets to the next station up the line and sat on the train looking innocent.

'We gotta change at Richmond', Johnny said after a while.

I was just going to ask why when I tumbled – 'You crafty ol' bugger.' I grinned at him. 'The North London Line – of course! Brilliant – yer not just a pretty face are yer mate!'

At Richmond we scuttled across the platform on to the waiting Broad Street train. The next bit was dodgy – we had to pay the ticket collector at Highbury, claiming we'd got on only a couple of stations before. Our luck was holding, however, for Highbury Station was deserted. It had been bombed and was now a ghost station echoing to the sound of our hobnailed boots as we walked along the platform and out on to the street. I could hardly believe our luck. We arranged to meet the following afternoon for the return journey.

Outside on the pavement, the sense of freedom, even at Highbury Corner, was pure magic. It was just like mature wine – intoxicating – and there was just time for a quick one before going our separate ways.

'Gotcher socks ready for darnin?' I asked Johnny, grinning.

'Yeah', he replied, "ow did yer guess', wiping his lip and leaning back on the bench. We parted outside, Johnny heading for Cissbury Road in Tottenham, me jumping on a 43 bus to the Archway and home to surprise Mum and Dad. While Mum made me a cuppa, Dad looked me up and down with an old soldier's professional eye, wanting to know all the details of my time away.

That night I went down to the Bunk, met some old mates and spent most of the evening with them and Ginger Charlesworth, who was home on leave from the Merchant Navy. Ginger and I picked up a couple of birds in the Clarence pub and we ended up at Lower Edmonton, where their front door was shut firmly in our faces after a brief goodnight kiss.

'Bloody dead loss that was', grumbled Ginger, as we stumbled back to the High Road in the blackout. We found a bus stop after some searching but it soon became obvious that nothing was running – it was well after midnight by then.

'I suppose its Shanks's pony', he sighed, as we started our long walk back along the High Road.

'I'm goin ter check their bleedin' addresses the next time I pick up a bit of skirt – locals only', I muttered.

After a few minutes Ginger spotted a glow in the sky. 'Hey look, Boysie, it's a fire.'

'Yer've gotta be kidding', I said, looking in the direction he indicated.

'No, I tell you – it's a bloody fire. Come on let's get crackin'.'

We both ran towards the glow, and as we turned the corner we were faced with the full impact of the fire. It was in a timber yard and it was well ablaze – there wasn't a soul to be seen.

'What the f...ing 'ell are we goin ter do', I shouted above the noise of the fiercely burning wood.

'Find one of those red fire alarms.' Luckily one wasn't far away and we both tried to smash the glass window protecting the alarm handle. I tried to break it with my elbow, but only succeeded in bruising my funnybone. Ginger had a bash at it with no luck. I hit it with the heel of my boot – smash, the glass flew everywhere.

'Pull the bleedin 'andle', yelled Ginger.

'I 'ave, I 'ave – what do we do now?' I said as I put my boot back on again.

'Dunno', said Ginger. 'I suppose we better wait 'ere.' After a few minutes silence he said 'Yer know, its a bit dodgy standing 'ere Boysie. Clear sky and all – this thing's like a bleedin beacon, could 'ave bombs droppin' any moment.'

'It's all clear', I retorted. 'Come on, let's see if we can get the gates open.'

Before we could argue any further, we heard the clanging of the fire engines' bells in the distance and then much nearer as they screeched and thundered round the corner into the street. We waved and the first one stopped right by us.

'You pulled the alarm?' asked the fireman.

We nodded.

'Jump aboard', the driver shouted. We did and had a brief but exciting ride to the blaze. It was getting out of control by now, the smoke and flames making the atmosphere hot to breathe but – strange – no other local people there. The fireman hacked the gates open with axes while others coupled hoses up to a hydrant nearby.

'Come on you two, give us a hand to carry the hose.'

We were obviously regarded as a part of the team.

One fireman dumped a reel of firehose in my arms. 'Get it over there and couple it up to that one.' I gasped as the full weight of the hose hit me, knees sagging from the weight as I staggered over and with a struggle joined the brass couplings together. I unrolled the hose – sweating and exhausted by now in the heat of the burning timber. As water began to flow through the hoses it sprayed out from the couplings and soaked us as we carried more hoses up to the front. 'What a bloody mess' I thought grimly – I was soaked by now with a combination of sweat and cold water and my uniform was covered in mud from where I had stumbled more than once trying to unroll the hosepipe.

After battling for what seemed ages to control the fire, the leading fireman came over and thanked us both for our help.

'Don't mention it' replied Ginger, cheerful still even though soaked and scorched like me. 'Anytime!'

By now groups of local people were standing around in dressing gowns, curlers and slippers watching the scene. We turned to continue our plod home, and slowly ambled the four miles that still separated us from our beds – past Tramway Avenue, not a tram in sight – following the tramlines home. We discussed the pros and cons of hijacking a tram, deciding against it when we realised neither of us could drive one. Ginger, who was on legitimate leave from the Merchant Navy and who had had a more than exciting time on convoy duty in the North Atlantic during the past six months, echoed my thoughts at one point as we walked wearily past the silent Spurs football ground. 'Be glad to get back fer a bleedin' rest!' I was inclined to agree with him.

I arrived home in the early hours and slept late on Sunday morning. I had a bath and a snack and spent some time cleaning up my uniform. After checking to see everything was OK in the mirror I lit a fag, had a few words with Dad about the events of the night before and shot off to meet Johnny at Highbury Station, still aching from the exertions of firefighting.

Jumping off the 43 bus I saw Johnny waiting anxiously for me.

'Had a good time?', he said, 'anything exciting?'

'Nah Johnny, just a family drink at the pub.' I was too tired to elaborate. We walked down the station stairs onto the desolate platform and a train rumbled in after a 10 minute wait. At Richmond we kept a very low profile before catching the connecting train.

We got back to barracks OK but it wasn't long before I was in trouble again. I had been issued with some brand new kit to replace some I had lost and the new webbing, such as belt and gaiters, would not take the blanco (cleaning powder) properly. It needed several applications of the stuff to look right and I didn't have the time. I went on parade with decidedly patchy webbing and of course was soon the object of scrutiny. The eagle-eyed officer sentenced me to six pack drills for my efforts, which meant turning out in full kit for an hour each evening until they decided you had learned your lesson. Kit on these occasions had to be spot on or you had to keep coming back until they were satisfied.

'Sodding pack drill', I fumed, as we changed kit back in the barrack room.

'Never mind Boysie', said Bill, a regular soldier from the next bunk. 'Borrow my gear, I've passed muster wiv' these ever since I joined up.'

'Ta Bill – y're a pal. 'Ave a couple of snouts.'

'You can't go wrong with these', he affirmed, as he handed his kit over to me. I lined up with the other defaulters and stood to attention on the parade ground for the drill that evening. Passing the inspection was a foregone conclusion in my mind. I could see the gleaming brasses in the periphery of my vision as the officer and sergeant drew level. After a cursory glance: 'Dirty brasses' I couldn't believe it! That meant I'd got another drill to do on top of the others – it took me a fortnight to get off that bloody pack drill and I reckoned I only got passed in the end because he got sick of my face. He was one of the duty officers we disliked intensely because of his petty mindedness. It was nothing to do with substandard presentation of kit except in the original instance. To prove my point, I hadn't touched Bill's kit from the night before – there was no need – in order to get the final OK. I really resented that because it meant getting dressed in full kit each evening and being on parade during our limited and precious free time.

Church parades on Sundays were another occasion for being dressed up in best uniform. We lined up on the square in contingents according to our religions. The C of E was by far the biggest. If you were a Methodist or Nonconformist it was just your bad luck – you were C of

E as far as the Guards were concerned. I did wonder once where they would send any Jew who joined – but that situation never arose, so the answer is still a mystery to me. Each group went their various ways – the only time we were separated out within the platoon. A couple of my mates were RCs and Cliff, of course, was a Sally Army man.

We marched down to Holy Innocents Church minus rifles. In the church the front benches were occupied by the officers and us lot were in the rear, separated from the officers by a few benches of service women. It was a fine garrison church whose walls were draped by ancient battle honours, some so old that they were colourless and beyond repair.

In the NAAFI after church we would enjoy a cuppa and a wad if we could afford it and plan what we were going to do with our remaining free time. Cliff, Harry, Les and I would often do the town after dinner to see what the talent of Windsor could offer. An additional entertainment was in spotting the twisters, as the RSM had called them. Sometimes we watched them beering up a Guardsman before they disappeared, singly, out of the pub door. They were from all walks of life – no class distinction there, it seemed, unlike the well defined distinction within the Guards of officers and men, neither group associating with the other.

One of the old sweats from the barracks had it made, as he told us one Sunday. 'Beer never costs you a penny if you know the ropes', he said over a full pint glass. Max was 6ft 2, blue eyes, hairy chest and close cropped hair – what we would call 'butch' nowadays.

'Leave off', I scoffed disbelievingly. 'They don't give all that beer away fer nuffin'.'

'Straight up', assured Max in his gravelly voice. 'Yer just squeeze their bum friendly like when it's your turn to buy', he said, as he got up to buy a round.

'Get out of it! – Yer havin' us on!', protested Johnny.

'True.' replied Max. 'You get to know them by the way they dress and hold themselves – some, like that one over there', indicating with his eyes, 'even wear make up and scent and call themselves girls' names. I tell you what, Boysie, if I sees yer in the pub in Peascod Street I'll introduce yer.'

'No thanks Max. I don't fancy me 'and round some poofter's arse, that's fer sure! That's worse than a knee trembler at the pictures. I'll leave the nancy boys to you old uns.'

'Cheeky young bugger', replied Max, with a good-natured grin. 'Yer don't know what yer missin' – all that free beer!'

Our lack of money severely limited our beer purchasing power, so the four of us would often just stroll around Windsor, through the riverside gardens and across the Thames onto the Brocas. This gave us the opportunity of eyeing the talent, and we used to split off if we landed a girl that took our fancy, meeting up again in the cafe opposite the barrack gates for our usual sausage sandwich or beans on toast and another cuppa. It was a funny little cafe – like someone's front room rather than the normal commercial establishment. That was probably half its charm – it was homelike. We loved the place and its grub.

Now and then we were lucky enough to be invited into local homes – a real luxury, as it usually meant free grub. But these occasions were rare. Food was scarce for everyone, and such invitations were few and far between.

On one of our tours of inspection Harry and I met two young sisters and were invited home for Sunday tea. We both polished ourselves up to the nines for the occasion and Harry gave the orders as usual. 'Now Boysie, leave the talkin' ter me.'

Passing through the barrack gates the corporal on duty gave us an old-fashioned look. 'We've bin invited out ter tea.' Harry volunteered a reply to the corporal's unasked question.

'Not to the Castle, I take it?'

'Not today, corp, just a little 'ouse down by the gasworks,' I replied, rubbing my bootcap up against the back of my trousers just in case he decided to be funny.

'Right – names?', he said, and we were on our way

We found the tiny terraced house and Harry knocked on the door. My knees were trembling. Going out to tea in this formal way was not part of my experience – in the Bunk you ate when you had enough money and that was it, entertainment was out. The girls opened the door and we were ushered into their front room where the table was laid for tea. In the corner was an old-fashioned upright piano which loomed large in the small room. The girls, Liz and Kate, stood there looking like a pair of dreams – identically dressed though they weren't twins. Kate, my bird, had lovely corn coloured hair, greenish eyes, a turned up nose and a semi-permanent grin which lit up her face. We were introduced to their parents and as we sat down to tea I felt terribly uneasy at getting my feet 'under the table' as they say. I was happy enough to let Harry do all the talking. We had winkles, shrimps and celery with bread and butter and cake to follow – goodness knows how they got hold of the stuff. I tucked in and made the most of it, trying to eat politely and not gorge myself. Every time I looked up the Mum's eyes seemed to be on me and this made me feel uncomfortable again. I had to undo the top eyehook of my tunic as my Adam's apple began to feel twice its usual size and I felt as if I was choking. Harry chatted on and on, scattering platitudes and polite small talk over the room, winking at me every now and then. He was thoroughly enjoying himself.

'More tea, Boysie?' said Mum as she hovered next to me with a large brown teapot. 'Strange name – Boysie', she said conversationally as she filled my cup.

'Yes – it's just a family nickname', I replied and the girls giggled. I was relieved when it was time to go – I had found it a slightly claustrophobic experience.

We left for Chelsea Barracks a few days later. The barracks were old and primitive but being back in London was great. We made the most of our opportunities to pub crawl around Sloane Square and the Kings Road.

There were awkward sods here too – one evening I was on my way out to see the latest bird when the corporal on duty at the gate looked me up and down. 'Dirty brasses – you can't go out like that', he said. I was livid and shot back to the barrack room to borrow a mate's belt and give my buttons a quick shine. When I got back to the gate the corporal was standing outside the guardroom in the gloom. As I hurried up he came towards me. 'You can't go out like that', he said – again. 'Dirty brasses.' It was quite dark by now so how the bloody hell did he know? I couldn't even *see* his brasses.

'Aw come on', I protested, as we went into the guardroom, 'Look corp, I'm on a promise with this date – do me a favour.' But no way was he going to let me out. As we stood there I noticed a mirror set in the floor and asked him what it was for.

'That's for the Jocks with them kilts', replied the corporal. 'They make them stand on that before they let them out to see if they're wearin' anythin' underneath.' I grinned, despite my fury at him. I couldn't believe it, but the corporal was quite serious.

I had a soft spot for Chelsea Barracks – they had stood there a good hundred years or so. When we did manage to get past the corporal at the gate we had plenty of entertainment and sports to choose from in the neighbourhood, being right in the heart of London. There were always girls hanging round the gates on Chelsea Bridge Road, as there had been at Minehead and Windsor. Some of the squaddies used to stand stark naked at the windows at the far end opposite Pimlico Road showing off their bodies and wedding tackle to the birds at the railings. A pair of boots slung at their backsides would soon put a stop to them and that would be the end of the show for the night.

We had great times. Harry was a dab hand at the pub piano and many an evening he hammered away on the keys, a full row of glasses sitting on top of the piano for him and the rest of us around him singing our heads off or snogging if we had picked up a bit of fluff. We looked after each other as we crawled round and generally had a ball.

The barracks had the best food yet and it was eaten in civilised surroundings too, with white tablecloths and little pots of flowers on the tables. The one fly in the ointment, apart from the inadequate ablution facilities, was the constant presence of the hated 'redcaps' – the military police – who were stationed in the same barracks.

Battersea provided us with our first experience of street fighting. We used the badly bombed Queens Road area to learn the techniques among the back yards, brick rubble, smashed houses and pubs and wrecked churches – a ready made battlefield area on our doorstep. We learned the realities of hand-to-hand combat, how to tackle a bayonet wielding enemy and how to swing from empty windows. We had the bombed out church as our last bastion and held its nave, now open to the sky, against all comers. An incongruous touch in this grim scene was the audience we had throughout – women just like Mum and her friends in turbans and floral print wrapovers, fags in mouths and carpet slippers, some with shopping bags and small kids attached. All complained of the noise, which woke the kids, and the dust and smoke, which made their washing dirty as it hung out to dry. They didn't seem to realise that these mock battles could so easily have been for real in their own back yards. Then they would have all been dead and past caring about dirty washing and wailing kids.

To get to and from Battersea we had to cross Chelsea Bridge. Believe me, it was easier going than coming back – by the end of the day we were knackered. How we had the energy to go pub crawling and flirting in the evenings I'll never know. It spoke wonders for our fitness, that's for sure!

Soon we were back again in Windsor but not at the Victoria Barracks. This time our platoon was stationed at a large and beautiful country house at Old Windsor, with the Thames – the constant companion of those days, it seems – at the bottom of the beautiful and spacious grounds. Our training at Windsor was complete and we now formed part of a holding battalion ready to go anywhere at any time.

While I was there I did my stint on guard duty and, true to form, I was soon in trouble again. While I was standing one evening a civilian rode towards me on a bicycle at a fair rate of knots. He made no attempt to stop so I stepped out, bayonet pointing forward and challenged. 'Halt. Who goes there?' The cyclist didn't seem to be expecting this and had to swerve violently to avoid riding straight into my bayonet. Unfortunately he swerved straight into a nearby tree! He got up and walked back towards me, purple with rage.

'You blithering idiot! Don't you know who I am?', he demanded.

'No, I don't', I replied, still covering him with my rifle.

'Well I'm the Sergeant Major. Take a good look at me and you'll know me next time!'

'But you're in civvies, sir', I replied, 'What if I let you through without a challenge? We've bin told to challenge all civilians ... Sir.'

'Humph' was all he said. Turning and picking up his bike – now with a badly dented front wheel – he walked off towards the house. I heard nothing more about that particular incident. There wasn't much he could have done anyway – I was only following orders.

Soon after I was on guard duty again – this time in the early hours, between two and four in the morning. I had been standing there some time, bored to distraction, when I heard a rustling in the bushes just a few yards away. It was very dark. The hairs stood up on the back of my neck and my hands gripped the rifle as I shouted, 'Halt. Who goes there?'

No reply – the rustling continued.

'Halt or I fire', I shouted, convinced it was the enemy, but before I could do anything a large hedgehog emerged from the bushes and trotted past me, completely unmoved by my threats. I retreated to the sentry box feeling a right fool.

We were never told where we'd be going next and assumed we would not be staying in this idyllic setting for long. Where would we be sent? We no longer regarded ourselves as trainees and as far as we were concerned, this time we were likely to be sent abroad at any time. The regiment had lost a lot of men in the North Africa campaigns and also at Anzio in Italy, in an attempt to cut off the Germans who held Monte Cassino at the time. But now the Battle of the Bulge at Bastogne in the Ardennes was raging and the Yanks had their backs to the wall trying to stem the onslaught as General Von Rundstedt's tanks smashed all before them trying to get to Antwerp. The US Commander and his encircled troops had been asked to surrender and his reply had been 'nuts'. But the Germans advanced so swiftly that they were taking non-combatant prisoners. It was a prolonged battle to push them back and the allies rushed up reinforcements to plug the gaps. We were expecting to be moved at any time to fill in the gaps in our battalions.

About this time I remember being on a weekend pass and drinking in the Russell Arms in Isledon Road with Ginger, my Merchant Navy mate who was also on leave – it was funny how our leaves seemed to coincide – and we weren't complaining. While we were chatting, a gunner in the Royal Artillery brought over a pint and placed it in front of me. I looked up wondering what was going on and trying to remember if I knew the bloke – but he was a complete stranger.

'This is for you, mate,' he said to me. 'I was at Longstop Hill in North Africa when your mob climbed that hill, captured it and handed it over to the Yanks who lost it again to the Jerries. Five times your lot took it and each time them bleedin' Americans lost it again. I take my hat off to your mob – it was important to 'old that ridge. They were great. This is my way of sayin' thanks.'

I was embarrassed yet very touched. 'That's good of yer, mate, but I wasn't there you know.'

'Don't matter mate – drink up', and he moved away.

I drank up – drinking to the lads who had impressed this gunner so much.

That evening we picked up a couple of ATS girls in the Medina, a pub on Seven Sisters Road. Both girls were stationed on the gun site in Finsbury Park where there were a few anti-aircraft guns. I don't know how effective these guns were – they made a lot of noise and scattered a lot of shrapnel over the surrounding area, but I often wondered how many planes they hit.

These thoughts were far from our minds that evening as we embarked on a pub crawl with our two girls. We started off from the Medina where Jimmy, Ginger's brother, knocked out tunes on the piano – he was a smashing pianist, playing requests as we crowded around and sang the words of a song or hummed. More than one free pint came our way – we never knew who from – but whenever I was the recipient I always felt embarrassed. The civilians were putting up with just as much hardship as we were.

At the end of the evening the four of us staggered back to the camp site in Finsbury Park still singing as we said goodbye. They told us not to get lost. Very funny – even in the pitch black we knew the park so well we could point our noses in the right direction and climb the gates beside the barrage balloon, no bother. The park itself was beautiful, especially in the autumn – wide sweeps of grass dominated by the boating lake and the bandstand, clumps of trees and the great cricket pitches over by the New River where many a good game had been won or lost. I felt that that leave might well be my last before....I didn't know what. But I remember savouring every moment of it.

When we were finally moved out, there was great curiosity and excitement but none of us had the foggiest idea where we were going. A couple of hundred or so of us were packed into a train at the crack of dawn one morning and eventually arrived at Waterloo. We formed up on platform 17 and in full battle dress and rifles were marched in threes through the packed station during the rush hour. We had to slow down because of the crowds until an old porter with one of those old-fashioned trolleys took charge.

'Stand clear. Stand aside', he hollered, as he pushed people to one side. 'Here comes the real soldiers.' People jumped aside and as we came up to him he stood to attention, cap on his chest.

'Real soldiers?', I thought. 'My God he means us!'

We marched out on to the road in front of the station where there were about ten 3-tonners waiting. We still knew nothing about our final destination. We were dismissed and ordered to get in the lorries. I caught sight of one of the RASC drivers, who looked familiar.

'Blimey, its Georgie! Hey Georgie – over 'ere mate', I called.

'Stone the crows, Boysie', replied the driver, coming over. 'What you doin' 'ere me ol' son?' – Georgie Forster had lived just around the corner from me in North London: we had sat next to each other at Pooles Park School.

'You're not takin' us are yer?' I queried.

'Yep – got orders to take you lot ter St Pancras.'

'What's a little tich like you doing driving a bloody great lorry like this?', I asked, delighted to see his red-haired bonce again. He laughed, his ginger hair crinkling under his beret.

'Yer in a right mob 'ere Boysie, All that bull!' He climbed up into the cabin and I pushed my way into the blokes in the back of his lorry.

'It's St Pancras for us lads', I announced. 'Make what yer like outa that – we're goin' North.'

4

Scotland

The train carriage gradually filled with smoke and stale air but we were quite happy. Blancoed kit was stowed in every available space.

'Anyone got a snout?', I tried to scrounge, having given my packet to Georgie at St Pancras station.

'Yeah – 'ave a Woodbine.'

'Ta, Bill. Looks like your countryside round 'ere, dunnit? What do they call it – the Black Country?'

'That's it', said Bill, who came from near Stoke. The train rattled on through Stafford as we played cards and chatted.

'I 'ope this train stops at a main station', said Jack. 'I wanna cuppa – I'm gasping.'

'You'd better ask the sergeant – 'es' just comin past now.'

'Any chance of this train stopping for us to get a cuppa, sarge?', said Jack. 'And while we're askin', where the bloody 'ell are we headin' for anyway?'

'Last I 'eard was Scotland.'

'I thought that was only a rumour.'

'Scotland! you've got to be kiddin us, sarge', Harry said in disbelief.

Gloom descended on us like a thick cloud. The card game we had been playing was forgotten as we discussed this news.

'Anyone ever been there?' Someone wanted to know. None of us had – as far as we were concerned it was no man's land.

'That's where the blokes wear skirts and no knickers, ain't it?'

'No chance of bunking off either, this bleedin' train's not going ter stop – not even for a cuppa', mourned Jack who had just come back from the khazi and had checked with the sergeant again. We peered out of the window and the carriage became unnaturally quiet as we sized up the situation and delved into our own thoughts.

I was getting very thirsty – we hadn't had a drink since breakfast, which had been before dawn, and now it was afternoon. We had each been given sandwiches – one meat and one cheese – but no drink.

''Ere Harry – see if the cook's goin ter brew up', I asked him, as he stood up.

'Why me?'

'You're the one with the gift of the gab – the patter – the charm.' I grinned at him.

'All right – I'll see what I can do.' Flattery never failed with Harry.

Just then one of the young lieutenants came by and we called him in – wanting to know more about our destination.

'Is it true we're goin' to Scotland, sir?'

'Yes, that's correct.'

'Whereabouts, sir?'

'A place called Stobbs Camp, it's up in the hills above Hawick', he replied. He tried to explain that we needed experience of that kind of terrain – but we didn't appreciate that point.

By now the countryside was getting bleak and hilly. We must have been well north by then – near the Lakes maybe. I didn't recognise any names in the stations we went through. I remember crossing a very high viaduct and soon after that we pulled in at a small station where a porter was bawling out 'Hoik, Hoik', as he walked along opening all the doors of the train. We had become very cramped after so long in the train and it was sheer luxury to get out and stretch and form up. The luxury was somewhat marred by the cold drizzle and mist that met us on the platform. Eventually we were all sorted out and the gear collected and we marched out of the station into the yard, depressed to our boots, hungry and more than a little thirsty.

'Hey, Warren' – I nudged the bloke next to me – 'you'll get none of yer fancy boys up 'ere – what are yer goin ter do, eh, me ol' china?'
He flung a small heavy pack at me. 'Do us a favour – turn it in Boysie – I'm suffering enough already – mind you those hairy knees and kilts look dinkie! Mama-mia, bung us a fag to steady me nerves.'

We looked around as we stood in the station yard – the drizzle and mist were still drifting in. In the distance we could see large buildings with many windows down in the valley close to the river.

'What's them factories over there, Harry?'

'Dunno Boysie', replied Harry. 'They look like woollen mills to me.'

'They look look like prisons ter me – or barracks.'

'Yeah', agreed Harry, as he looked closely at them. 'I see what you mean. They do a bit, don't they? Imagine doin' porridge in there – more like the Prisoner of Zenda I should imagine!'

A fleet of army lorries rumbled into the yard. We were all hoping that the camp wasn't too far out of town as a whistle was blown and we piled into the backs of lorries.

At last we arrived at Stobbs Camp. The mist had come right down as we climbed out of town and we could just make out a formation of nissen huts. What we could see only increased our gloom: they looked bloody primitive in the bad weather. When the mist lifted a little we could see an enclosure in the valley bottom surrounded by a high barbed wire fence. Inside the enclosure were loads of SS POWs, many of them washing clothes in horse troughs. We could tell by the number of distinctive black uniforms that they were members of the German SS. We all had a good look – this was our first experience of the enemy at close quarters. They looked hard and mean to me – they must have been cheesed off about being incarcerated in these wet and misty hills, but I didn't feel sorry for the bastards. One of our jobs was to guard this bunch – and they took some guarding. Even behind fencing, we sensed that they hadn't accepted defeat.

I had got separated from my mates in the lorries and had to go from hut to hut to find them.

As I pushed my way into one of the huts I was greeted by Reg, Mickey and Johnny and I cheered up again, especially when Johnny passed the fags around.

' 'Ere, what the bleedin 'ell is that at the far end?', I said as I caught sight of a dirty grey shape moving in through the door at the far end.

'It's a blinking sheep.'

'A sheep? What d'yer mean?'

'A sheep – you know, lamb chops and all that wool they got stuck on 'em!'

'Looks like they've got right of way through 'ere', said Johnny, as we watched a dirty old ewe trot through the hut, stopping only to leave some droppings by one of the bunks. The sheep seemed quite used to us and while we were there walked unconcernedly through the nissen huts, inevitably leaving their droppings or piss for us to clean up. 'They're trying to get their own back on us because of what we did to them at Exmoor!' I shouted.

Another big fat and dripping wet ewe lumbered in through the far door and squeezed past the stove in the middle of the room, raising hisses and an awful smell as her woolly coat touched the hot metal. I decided on action.

'I'll draw up a roster for cleaning up the turds and piss', I said, as I watched this one trot past my bunk.

'Leave me off the list, Boysie', replied Johnny, 'I'm allergic to sheep shit.'

'Oh yeah. You're first on my list mate – I'll get me own back for them bleedin' socks of yours yet. Cam on nah – no 'idin' behind them bunks. Coxy, Everett – lets be 'avin' yer.' I made a list of all the names in the hut.

'Say, Spiv' are you on that list?' Cooper wanted to know – scanning the list. 'Typical, Yer the last name on the bleedin' list!'

'So? At least I'm on it', I retorted, 'and when its my turn I'll padlock the bloody doors!'

The sheep continued to wander in and out completely undisturbed by the boots and other missiles aimed at them when they started dumping their turds on the floor. Let's face it, they were here before we were – it was their patch.

The next morning there was a great deal of interest in the scene outside. The mist had lifted and the hills showed up in their glory. On one of them there was carved a huge Scots Guards badge – the thistle standing out proudly from the cross. Other regimental crests had been dug in the soil, painted in the colours of their national flags. They must have taken a lot of work.

We soon settled into the routine of long marches, battle activities and practising manoeuvres and landings on St Mary's Loch. We always advanced carefully in lines, firing with bayonets fixed – it was all too easy for some laggard to shoot you in the arse.

We got down into Hawick as often as we could and drowned our sorrows in the local pubs. One of the high spots of the town as far as we were concerned was the fish and chip shop just by the bridge over the river.

Betty – the ATS girl on the gun site at Finsbury Park – wrote to me and suggested I visited her home in Galashiels and meet her sister. I was only too pleased. One Saturday I got an all-day pass, and caught the train to Galashiels. It was a pretty run past high hills, fast-flowing rivers and lush fields and woodland. I eventually found the house and Janet, Betty's sister, showed me into the house and gave me tea. Afterwards we went for a walk during which she pointed out various landmarks. Although I enjoyed myself I felt a bit like the twelfth man in the cricket team – the girl I really wanted to be with was nearly 400 miles away in London.

I was dressed up to the nines, complete with gloves, and on my best behaviour – but it was tough going as I had a hard time understanding her accent. I guessed mostly and smiled and nodded for the rest of the time. I'm sure the problem was mutual, as my thick Cockney accent wasn't any easier to understand. At one point I had to fight down a surge of laughter – this was when one of the nearby hills was pointed out and I was told it was called Maiden Paps – no prizes for guessing what we in the camp would soon have called it! I amused myself on the return journey wondering what a town-bred Cockney lad like me could have done for a living in the area. I suppose I must have been subconsciously thinking of a future with Betty here in her home territory, but I wasn't about to rush into any such decisions. Army life was too insecure and unsettling.

The routine at Stobbs Camp was pretty much the same as Windsor and Chelsea, boring and repetitive. We made good use of the swimming baths in the town and after a long session would make a dash for the lorry to get back. If you were left behind it meant an eight-mile slog, all up hill. Cricket was another activity that relieved the boredom – I put my name down as a fast bowler, claiming I had been one of the Northern Poly's team – the biggest name in local cricket I could think of at the time.

My chance for selection came in a trial match. I bowled the new ball at the batsman, a young lieutenant; it was a yorker and it shattered his stumps.

'Excuse me, umpire, I wasn't ready', whined the officer, staying put.

'Bollocks! He was.' I shouted furiously, directing my appeal to the umpire. He stood unmoving and then decided. 'No ball', he called. I couldn't believe it. 'You've got ter be kidding', I exploded, with arms outstretched as I ran up to him.

'No I'm not kidding. 'E's the boss, at the other end', replied the umpire. Then it made sense.

He hit me for four off the next ball by throwing his bat at the ball and caution to the wind. I bowled bouncers flat out at him for the remainder of the over. The first ball flew over his head, the next past his ears and the last under his nose. I then took myself off bowling, complaining of cramp. The officer called out 'unlucky bowler' as I retreated past him towards the boundary. The match fizzled out into a draw. After we had tea, we stowed all the cricket gear and ourselves onto the lorry and headed back to camp.

There was no love lost between us and the Polish troops who were also stationed in town. Orders were given for action one evening after a young Welsh Guardsman was stabbed in the back by a Polish soldier. 'I don't want to see anyone in camp tonight. Get me?' was the instruction. The message got round and we were ready – we took a very dim view of one our brigade being knifed by a bloody Pole. We all piled into town that night armed with bayonets and all sorts of weapons, bent on revenge – we hated the Poles even more than the SS prisoners. What really got up our noses was what we saw as the preferential treatment they received. There they were in the comfort of the town while we were up in the wilds – miles from the nearest pub or a pretty girl. Their habit of strutting around with a local girl on their arm didn't help either. With the SS prisoners at least we knew where we were. They were no better off than we were. The Poles were just as foreign but we were never sure of them. That was a problem.

Trouble soon flared up that night and the local police had to be reinforced to try to stop the punch up. Mind you, the Poles had got wind of our coming and a lot were confined to quarters. Funny though – no one seemed to be missing the next morning, so no one had been detained by the authorities.

We had to take turns in guarding the prisoners of war. I often hoped some of them would try to escape so that I could have a go at them. When I saw the way they were pampered, cycling around the countryside to their jobs on nearby farms – with the freedom that went with it – my blood boiled. We were aware of the barbaric treatment of our lads by the Japs especially, and the harsh conditions that existed in the POW camps run by the Italians and the Germans. Details filtered through the Guards grapevine and from friends in other regiments. We didn't spend much time worrying about it. If we were in a front line battle we assumed we'd win or die – surrender or capture was never contemplated as far as we were concerned. We couldn't imagine the British Tommy in captivity in Germany being allowed to roam the German countryside. I wanted to get hold of the blighter had who issued the order giving the German prisoners such privileges – and lay one on him.

'Good old War Office', I thought, 'are they really on our side?'

Every evening outside our nissen hut a Scots piper would tune up, blowing his pipes for all he was worth, a striking figure resplendently dressed in his kilt and khaki uniform, but the lads used to tell him to piss off and play his bagpipes elsewhere. We watched him one evening playing his pipes and likened him to the Monarch of the Glen, the way he stood on the hillside. After that, that's just what he was called.

It was while we were here that the news we had all been hoping for finally came through – peace had broken out in Europe. I felt a great surge of relief – we all did – and that night we celebrated by firing Verey flares and tracer bullets into the dark sky, lighting up the surrounding area. In the ghostly light of the flares we could see the German prisoners running to the fence, wondering what was happening. As the truth dawned we could see disbelief in their faces. Our shouting and laughter echoed in the valley, disturbing the usual silence of the place. Later we had a few beers in the NAAFI and began to consider what peace in Europe would mean for us.

The war was still raging in the Far East and we wondered if we would be sent there. The prospect didn't appeal to us – our height didn't suit us for jungle warfare and the area was on the other side of the world – not just across the channel. But we knew that in fact we were still at war – we didn't know then that the war in the Far East would finish only three months later.

The next day we attended a service of thanksgiving on the hillside, with the crows and the sheep as our companions.

One day we were told to stand by for an early call the next morning. The King was visiting Edinburgh and we had been detailed to stand in line in front of the crowds. The next morning we formed up for inspection in the glare of the headlights of the lorries that were to take us there. It was about 3 a.m. and we'd already been up an hour by then. One pace back and we'd disappear into the night!

Eventually we all passed muster, climbed aboard the lorries and a couple of hours later jumped stiffly out into the drizzly dawn on Princes Street. We lit fags and stretched our legs before getting into position. So this was Edinburgh.

'What a bloody turn up fer the books eh, Harry?', I whispered. There was no reply – Harry was fast asleep on his feet, propped up by his rifle. I squinted in Johnny's direction and Johnny, ever matter of fact, just stared ahead.

'What's this place called again?' he asked, gazing at Arthur's Seat.

'Edinburgh. It's the capital of Scotland.'

Just then we were called to attention. 'OK. Eyes front. Two paces to your right. Arm's length. Square up.' When we had finished shuffling and checking our lines, the grim faced sergeant cheered us up no end by informing us that we were in for a long wait.

As time wore on, more and more people gathered on the pavements and we got more and more bored and fed up.

'Can yer see any decent crumpet?' I hissed over to Harry.

'No.'

We must have been overheard, even though we stood a couple of feet out from the pavement, for just moments later some bird whispers in my ear that she'd be in a pub (whose name I forget) in Rose Street, later on! The message must have got around: in the next few minutes, first one girl then another was whispering rendezvous locations and arrangements in our ears! We couldn't see them as we couldn't turn our heads, but we chatted them up easily enough – like a pair of ventriloquists' dolls. Johnny could only look on in dismay – he'd missed his chance! I signalled with my hand to Harry that I had five invitations. Not to be outdone Harry grinned and tapped his rifle butt on the ground seven times to denote his score. Unbelievable! Twelve birds between the two of us, in little more than fifteen minutes, and we didn't even turn our heads. Several other men in the platoon had scored. You could tell by the way they were smiling.

The procession started and we stood rigid presenting arms; by now both sides of Princes Street were packed and every window too – we could hear the voices above us rather than behind us. I was starving and beginning to feel faint, trying to keep my mind occupied by looking closely at the scene around me. On the right from where I stood was what I took to be a large block of tenements perched on a rocky hill. This, I found out later, was Edinburgh Castle, but at the time I wondered why on earth they had built a block of council flats in such an inconvenient place.

Just then the King went by. I reckoned that we had been standing or travelling for about twelve hours with no proper meal. I cheered myself up while we awaited orders to stand easy by thinking of the prospects of the twelve dolly birds that were waiting, hoping they were good lookers.

We ate our sandwiches and had a welcome brew up as the crowds dispersed. We were in high spirits, looking forward to meeting the girls. But alas, the best laid plans ... As we finished eating, the order to get back on board the waggons was given by a red-faced corporal who shrieked out the command in a loud high-pitched voice that made anyone within twenty feet wince. We were appalled. ' 'Ere, Corp', we remonstrated 'We've got some nice young ladies to meet outside Woolworths and Jenners. It's all bin fixed up!'

'Nope, sorry mate', he said in a more normal voice. 'Orders from the adjutant', and marched off.

We looked at each other in disbelief.

'The first time we get some civilised company for yonks and this happens', moaned Harry as he clambered back into the lorry.

'Yeah. I suppose it's back to bloody sheep land', I replied, sick with fury and disappointment, I could imagine those twelve dolly birds pacing up and down Princes Street and Rose Street waiting for us – what a waste of talent, and there wasn't even a chance to let them know we couldn't make it.

Even worse was to come. When we got back to camp we discovered that Hawick had been put out of bounds by the Colonel because of the situation with the Polish troops. If I remember rightly it was those sods that we had gone to war for in the first place! The only consolation was that we had already got our own back and given them a right pasting.

I had had my fill of marching, crawling and humping night and day through the forests, bogs and heathland, getting soaked and pretty near drowned in the lochs, so I volunteered for one of the jobs at the officers' mess. It was a nice little number, plenty of grub and a darned sight easier on the feet and most other parts of the body.

Despite the easy job and the grub, I wasn't getting anywhere and it soon became monotonous. I was restless too, so when volunteers were asked to staff the British War Crimes Executive I offered my services. It was a very hush hush affair – no one could find out details – which made it seem all the more attractive to me at the time.

Sitting on my bed polishing my rifle butt a few days later Harry came over and sat on the next bed. 'I hear you've volunteered for the BWCE job, Boysie! What d' you go and do that for?'

'Don't really know, 'Arry', I replied.

'Hey, Boysie, who's goin' ter darn yer socks now, mate', piped up Johnny, as he looked over his 'tupn'y blood' comic.

'Good question, Johnny. G'is yer address and I'll send 'em to yer missus.'

'Trust you to have the answer', he grinned.

Some time later six of us in all, two from my company and four from the rest of the 3rd battalion, just back from overseas, reported for briefing for the BWCE job. We were given embarkation leave – and we knew for the first time that we were going overseas.

5

The Journey of Sorrows

We began our journey one evening full of high spirits. We had been dumped at the station by a truck and we were on our own, with a couple of days' leave ahead. Although we all lived in different parts of the country, we all had to get the London train to begin with. Six of us – Jacko, Freddie, Bill, Peter, Jughead and me – headed for God knows where. The train shuffled round the bend a few minutes later, and we all clattered aboard.

The first to leave the train was Freddie, who was going to Middlesbro' and got off at Carlisle. Bill and Jughead were heading for the South-west – Somerset and Cornwall respectively – and after a while I was the only one left. The others had got off in the Midlands somewhere. As I walked out of Euston Station, the capital was just waking up, and people were scurrying to work. I headed for home.

It was the first time I had been in London since the war in Europe had ended. Nothing much had changed – the bombed buildings were still there. I suppose the main difference was the absence of blackouts and expectation of a peaceful night's sleep. I thought of all those who had died and wondered if there would be a memorial to them – St Paul's Cathedral would be the proper place, I thought.

The leave soon finished. It was pouring with rain as I caught the tube to the Railway Headquarters building on Marylebone Road. It was being used as a transit camp, and, compared with the ones I was to stay in later, it was like a five star hotel. I was the last of our sextet to arrive.

'Get yourself a couple of blankets, Boysie', said Freddie as he caught sight of me. 'We've saved you a space – we've got to stay together.'

'Yeah? Okay, Fred', I replied as I looked round the packed hall. The place was crammed with servicemen – they were everywhere.

Bill, who was the oldest and had assumed the role of leader, told us that we'd better get some shuteye, as we had to be ready to leave at 3 a.m. A van was calling to pick us up and deliver us to Croydon airport. I was really keyed up – I had never been in an aircraft before.

We drove through the quiet streets, still glistening after heavy rain, and I remember crossing one of the bridges across the Thames and the seemingly endless miles of streets before we turned into the gates of the aerodrome. It was exciting to be there. I had watched newsreels of Amy Johnson and other aviator pioneers like Jean Batten and Charles Kingsford-Smith as they either landed or took off. Now I was about to take off too.

A couple of civilians met us and as we dismounted from the lorry I looked over and saw a Dakota standing nearby. Within minutes we were climbing aboard, helped by an RAF bloke. We sat on long wooden benches built along the fuselage, all very basic and spartan. The ribs of the aircraft stuck into your back and you had to make the best of it – no air hostesses or free champagne on this trip – not even parachutes!

The old warhorse of a plane charged down the runway, picking up speed, and soon we were airborne – I relaxed a bit and resumed breathing. I stopped again when a crew member came along with a spanner to tighten some nuts on the port side. 'Just screwing the wings back on', he joked.

The noise and vibration were something else. They stopped any conversation and all sleep. After a while I twisted round and peered out of the window – we were crossing the Channel and drawing close to the French coast. I remember seeing a few military vehicles dotted around on the quiet sandy beaches and wondering if this was Dunkirk. I imagined what it must have been like on that beach during the evacuation as men scrambled into boats of all kinds, up to their necks in water as the Stukas dive-bombed them.

Eventually we got sufficiently used to the noise to doze fitfully as we flew over northern France and Belgium and into Germany, where we landed on a makeshift air strip of wire mesh laid on grass, at the RAF station near Buckeburg, a short distance from Minden.

"Ere we are lads', I announced, as we struggled to our feet and collected our wits and gear: 'Germany.'

We were glad to get out and stretch and take in a bit of fresh air – one or two of us had felt queasy and we needed to walk around, a little shakily at first, until we perked up. Bill led us to the RAF cookhouse where we scrounged a cuppa. Once we'd got that down us we could consider our next move. We learned that we were to stay at a nearby house and wait for further orders. As we were settling in we were joined by a Royal Artillery sergeant who was going to travel with us as far as our next stop.

As we had time to spare we decided to go into Minden and explore. I was all eyeballs as we strolled around, for this was my first glimpse of Germany – a country I had heard plenty about in the past few years. The scars of war and bombing were only too obvious, no matter which way you turned. It was a depressing sight.

We still had no real idea what our trip was all about or our final destination, and we hung around on tenterhooks for a couple of days in the house, passing the time as best as we could. Finally we were told that a truck would pick us up the next morning. It duly arrived, driven by an RASC bloke, and the lot of us, including the RA sergeant, piled aboard. Only then were we told that we were going to Bad Oyenhausen – Monty's place.

When we got there the place was swarming with military – not a civilian to be seen. Where they had gone to was anybody's guess. It was a British Army camp now – nothing but khaki. The place was policed by the redcaps, who directed traffic as well as their more usual jobs, waving on the convoys of lorries and staff cars and the motor bike despatch riders who roared to and fro.

When we had settled into our billets the sergeant escorted us to the nearest bar and stood us a beer each.

'Good on yer sarge', I said.

'Don't worry son, it's only lent' he winked. 'You lot can pay for the next call.'

The billet at least was comfortable. Thinking that this was our final destination, here at the 21st Army Headquarters, we congratulated ourselves on what a cushy number we had landed. We sauntered over to the mess rooms, carrying our mess tins and mugs, and lined up to be served with stew and rice pud. As we sat at one of the trestle tables we agreed that the food wasn't too bad. While we waited for Bill to finish I looked around and noticed that the table nearby was being wiped down by what I assumed to be a German girl in a white overall and a turban. I turned and slapped her bum as she bent over the table. I grinned at her as she turned and the next thing I knew a greasy wet cloth was slung round my head, much to the amusement of my mates. I was told in a broad scouse accent to keep my so and so mitts to myself! These were no frauleins – they were the ATS girls, looking very different in the cookhouse gear to the smart girls on parade in their uniforms. The lads were still laughing at my embarrassment – and it was the end of a fine romance.

Later that afternoon we had a visit from a sergeant in the Intelligence Corps who told us where we were going – we were to be driven to a place called Nuremburg, near Munich.

The next day there we were – the five of us in the back of the waggon and Jacko in the front. Out of the gates the waggon rumbled, straight into a long convoy of lorries – big gun carriers – the lot. Our driver was a chirpy bloke, full of wisecracks. He immediately set about getting the waggon out of the hold up. He turned right down a side street then left and left again – smack into the convoy again! After several moves of a similar nature we eventually gained the open road, to everyone's relief, and for a while made good speed. Not for long though: after a few miles we were stopped in our tracks by a river.

'It's the Rhine', someone murmured, as we pulled back the flap and gazed out at the remains of the bridge that once spanned it.

Whatever it was called, it was very wide. The bridge and the land in the immediate vicinity must have taken a hell of a pasting – bomb craters and devastation everywhere.

'There must have been a pitched battle 'ere', Jughead muttered. We had to backtrack and make for the next crossing point, which we could see in the distance. We passed some abandoned German Tiger tanks on the way and pulled over to inspect them. They were enormous. The length of the gun barrel was unbelievable – the 88mm type, with a terrific range. One had its tracks blown off and another tilted over the edge of a ditch at a crazy angle. As I stood there I couldn't help thinking how much all that scrap metal would fetch in Flockie's scrap yard back home in Pooles Park.

We got back aboard and crossed the river over a huge Bailey bridge – a network of metal and wood – a typically marvellous Royal Engineer's job which safely carried all kinds of traffic over the swirling water. It seemed a long way across in our little truck as we bumped rhythmically over wooden sleepers. Below us were huge half-submerged barges sticking out of the river. They had been used to ferry troops across at one time but now they were like huge coffins in a river graveyard. All that remained of the original bridge were shattered stumps of masonry at either bank. All along our route, derelict and abandoned military vehicles were scattered around like huge carelessly discarded Dinky toys.

It was mid afternoon and we were travelling along a tree lined road. At one point it passed through a large wood, very quiet except for the sound of the waggon as it bounced and bucketed its way over potholes and ruts, slinging us about in the back. A thin fog drifted in between the trees and suddenly in the mist we spotted a high barbed wire compound. As we got nearer we could see small wooden huts on high stilts – observation posts, I supposed. We stopped, hoping to scrounge a cuppa, and entered by the main gate. We had gone only a few yards inside the compound when we were approached by an old man dressed in a pyjama-like suit of grey and green stripes. The appearance of this old man stopped us in our tracks. He could hardly stand on his tottering legs; he was filthy, with matted hair, stubble on his chin and sore red eyes. His cheekbones stuck out above hollows where his cheeks had once been. He muttered something in German, holding out his hands in a begging gesture, but we didn't understand what he said. Had we wandered into a POW camp?

Bill shouted for others to come out, hoping to find who was in charge, and a few dishevelled figures appeared from the huts. 'Gawd' said someone quietly as these apparitions shuffled closer. It was beginning to dawn on us what this place was – there was an air of something indefinable about it – a sense of desolation and, above all, a smell. We looked at these poor sods, little more than skin and bone, some with no hair, all barefoot and dressed in striped outfits, either shirtlike shifts or suits. Their eyes were sunken and their faces expressionless, but those eyes held fear, curiosity and hunger. One or two had a blankness that suggested that they had seen and been through just too much.

In a combination of English, sign language and halting German we questioned the first old man and eventually established that this had been a concentration camp and that these were the only survivors, left to fend for themselves. We asked where the others were. 'Todt' was the reply and they took us over to the far side of the camp and showed us a large pit half full of human bodies in varying stages of decomposition. There had been an attempt to cover the bodies with soil and white powder, quicklime I suppose, but the job had been left uncompleted. The smell was overpowering. We looked at each other in horror and someone began to vomit. We moved away hurriedly and searched the camp for the other survivors but found nothing. We didn't need sign language to find out what had been going on – our eyes told us the grisly details.

'The f...in' bastards', someone said, and that really said it all.

We gave them the cigarettes and chocolate we had on us and the water we had left in our water bottles. One of them wanted to know who we were. They had relaxed by now, sensing that we meant no harm.

'Tommies', I replied.

The bloke seemed to search his mind. 'Tommee?' he repeated. 'Ach, der Tommee, ja, ja.'

We explained that we were going to get help for them and left, leaving the gates wide open. It seemed that this particular camp had been overlooked and the inmates hadn't the strength to move out. We got into the waggon, shocked, nauseated and with a new awareness of what the war had meant to people unfortunate to have been subjected to Nazi rule. Jughead said that he had read somewhere that Himmler had been caught near Belsen, one of these camps.

By now dusk had fallen and we headed for the nearest town and transit camp as fast as we could, to report what we had found. That done we could then sort out where we were going to sleep that night.

For once I don't think any of us were too concerned with any grub. A stiff drink, yes – but grub – no thanks.

Eventually we pulled up outside what looked like a bombed church hall or factory – I'm not sure which – where we were to kip down for the night. We signed for a couple of blankets apiece from a bespectacled corporal and trod carefully among the tightly packed camp beds, each of which held a sleeping squaddie. The place was airless and smelt awful and I couldn't sleep for a long time. The smell in the hall reminded me of death, decay and dead bodies, of what I had seen that day, and I was nauseated by it and longed for daytime when we could get away.

The next morning when we went to the washrooms to wash and shave the scene made our guts churn. The place was filthy: the wash basins had been used as lavatories and were like the rest of the place – covered in shit. As we went to the mess room for breakfast I noticed a lot of men in Polish uniforms, speaking in their native tongue and totally unintelligible. I remembered seeing them in Scotland and asked the corporal about them, who told me that they were sleeping rough in the place. We blamed the Poles for the mess in the toilets and wash-basins – we'd heard similar tales at Hawick about their habits. Far better kipping in the open than these poxy transit camps, we thought. I asked the corporal what the stink in the place was. He reckoned we had been sleeping on a large burial pit where bodies had been slung in and covered in soil.

We were glad to leave the place and as we handed in the blankets to the corporal – complete with their complement of bugs and fleas – I told him to get a squad of Poles up to the ablutions with some disinfectant and mops and buckets to clean up the mess.

At the first small river we came to we stopped and had a strip wash and shaved. As we splashed around we saw streams of displaced persons shuffling along the roadside. Some pushed their worldly possessions along in battered prams or handcarts and bikes, others had only the clothes they stood in – whole families on the move. Most carried their bundles wrapped in a sheet or a blanket. No doubt tired and hungry, they staggered along, dragging their feet as they went past us, the children trying to get lifts on the handcarts. Where they were going to nobody knew. Were they escaping from the Russians? It looked like they had come a long way by the state of them, but we couldn't offer food as we had none ourselves. We motored on and stopped once for a brew up, the driver using the water from the van's radiator and what was left in our water bottles. It tasted good.

'Any idea where we are, mate?' I asked – we didn't know his name.
'Call me Steve', he said.

'OK Steve. Any idea where we are?'

'I think we're about here', he replied, pointing to a place on the map. 'According to the map, this road we're on goes in the right direction.' The other guys were content not knowing, but as usual I had wanted to know the whys – and in this case, the wheres.

For the next few hours we threaded our way through the laden handcarts and prams and took another high road. We came upon another concentration camp just like the last one, just as grim, set below the road in the forest. We had to summon up our courage to tackle the locked gates after the last camp. We forced the gate open and went from hut to hut calling out, but there was no response. There was no sign of life, but the same smell of death lingered about the place. We came to the conclusion that they were all dead or had been released by advancing troops. So we tied the gates open and drove off.

Late in the afternoon we approached a town that seemed completely devastated – as if there had been an earthquake. Steve slowed right down as we drove in – up and down the van lurched over bricks and lumps of old window frames along the potholed and cratered remains of a street. There wasn't a living soul to be seen. Everything, stick, stone and even metal, was twisted and torn and flattened, a maze of destruction. This was, or had been, Warburg – I had noticed a dust-covered sign in old German which gave its name. After several detours to bypass blocked streets we came to a halt. We were completely lost and all we could see was rubble in all directions.

Freddie and Jughead ambled along the road towards a bombed-out factory while we scouted the rest of the terrain, scrambling over masonry, slipping as we climbed to a high vantage point, but we still couldn't see a way out – other than the way we had come. All the roads looked blocked. Freddie and Jughead by now had got higher than us and were pointing in an easterly direction. They returned to the truck covered in dust and plaster; it took a great deal of slapping and brushing down to make them look respectable again. 'You two look like a pair of ghosts', I muttered, keeping punching distance away from them.

It was a claustrophobic place, like a huge maze of devastated brickwork. Steve manoeuvred the van through gaps and around bends, aiming in the general direction Jughead and Freddie indicated. Luckily they were right and after an anxious half hour or so we emerged dusty and mightily relieved on the outskirts of what remained of the town. We had seen no one. It was a new and unpleasant experience that left us unnaturally silent for a while.

There were no signposts, but the surface of the road was reasonable – it looked very like an autobahn. Steve pressed down on the accelera-

tor and we made good speed in the dusk. Suddenly we could hear singing and a jeep drew alongside.

'Hiya, buddies', the driver shouted over.

'Blimey – they're Yanks! Ride 'em cowboy', someone yelled.

'Well, doggone I'll be damned – it's the Limeys! Whadya know fellas', shouted a GI sitting in the back of the jeep. One of the Yanks
started singing 'It's a Long Way to Tipperary' and we joined in as the
two army vehicles raced side by side along the road. One of the GIs
leaned out and tossed a bottle over towards us.

'Hey, fellas – a present from Uncle Sam!' The bottle hit the side can-
vas of our lorry and fell onto our kitbags. The jeep accelerated away as
we thanked them with the thumbs up sign.

'Can you beat that?', I shouted. 'What a turn up for the books.'

Fred examined the bottle: 'It's whisky, lads!'

We wasted no time in toasting Uncle Sam with swigs from the bottle.

Finally, late that evening, we reached the outskirts of Nuremburg –
the centre of things. The streets were busy with American vehicles,
and refugees still crowded the pavements with their bundles. They
made an odd contrast with the brash, well-fed Yanks.

We had been instructed to report to the Grand Hotel, but the town
had been badly damaged, so all we could do was follow the tramlines,
believing – rightly as it turned out – that they would lead to the town
centre and that the Grand Hotel would be somewhere in the central
part too.

At last we pulled up outside a large building. We couldn't remember
the name of the bloke we had to report to – nor could we find the piece
of paper on which we had written it. We were getting more than a little
fed up and hungry by now. We had asked any number of GIs where the
Grand Hotel was but none of them seemed to know. In the end I asked
an old German – I stood there and said as loudly as I could 'Grand Hotel.' He looked hard at me and after a moment pointed in the direction
we were facing. He said nothing, but his piercing pale blue eyes said
much. I, too, said no more but I gave him a cigarette, he accepted it, we
shook hands, he nodded and pointed out the way again.

We eventually found the hotel, walked into the foyer and over to
the reception desk. The old boy at the desk spoke good English and we
asked for the British officer. He scanned his register and said 'There's a
Captain Lawson'; we nodded in agreement. He rang his room and told
us to wait across the hall. A few minutes later the officer came over to
greet us and introduced himself.

'You're all here then', he said with a smile of welcome. He was tall
and dark and on his shoulder was the green and white insignia of the
Intelligence Corps.

'I want you to go straight to Zirndorf. It's a small village about six miles away.' We groaned silently. He told Steve how to get there and said that we might be able to get a meal there.

Gum-chewing Yanks hung around the hotel foyer and the reception desk, their transatlantic accents echoing across to where we stood. The well-dressed receptionist was checking his register for a couple of very tasty American army women, while the hotel bell hops stared at our khaki uniforms, wondering where we had sprung from – they looked like they had just come out of the Hitler Youth brigade with their blond hair and blue eyes. We saluted the intelligence officer and made our way back to the waggon. The American sentry at the door had a large figure 1 on his sleeve as well as the number 28, which I later discovered was the 28th Infantry Division of the American First Army. 'So long, take it easy fellas', he drawled in his soft voice.

'You betcha mate', Jacko replied, as we reached the waggon which Steve had parked right outside the front door.

'Well chaps, it's home and don't spare the hosses', said our pint-size driver. We had nearly arrived!

6

Zirndorf

It was late by the time we arrived in Zirndorf. Now all we had to do was find the house where we were to sleep, but it took some finding: it was tucked away in a cul de sac at the edge of the village. Eventually we found it and thankfully climbed out, stretching our aching limbs before getting our gear out of the waggon. A sergeant in the Intelligence Corps came out to meet us and escorted us to the last house in the row. Because of the lateness of the hour he also left us some grub and tea so that we could make ourselves a meal. The food was eminently forgettable, but the cuppa we brewed was welcomed. Before he left the sergeant told us we'd be staying there for two or three days before being allocated to other houses in the village to prepare them for arrival of the British legal and military top brass who were arriving for the trials.

The next morning the sergeant returned and gave us a few details of our mission. We were the advance guard for the British staff involved in the International Military War Trials. Nuremburg, despite being extensively damaged, had been chosen as the location for the trial of the top ranking prisoners who had served in the Nazi government under Adolf Hitler. These trials were to be held in the Palace of Justice by British, French, American and Russian judges and other legal personnel. So there we were – a sextet of guardsmen, fed up with the sheep, rain and isolation in Hawick, who had volunteered for special duties and who were now about to be thrown into the international hurly burly of the most famous trial since the Dreyfus affair.

When we had sorted ourselves out we set out to find the Cafe Bub, which was run by the American Army and where arrangements had been made for us to eat. We had to walk to the village as Steve had returned to Bad Oyenhausen early that morning. The RC church was on the corner then the road dipped down a hill. On the left-hand side was a large building labelled Gymnasium standing in its own extensive grounds with a football pitch and a running track. For a long time this had me puzzled – I couldn't make out why a small village like this one had such a large gym. Only much later did I discover that a German gymnasium is a school.

Just beyond the level crossing at the bottom of the hill we found the

Cafe Bub and bowled in. I had been elected mouthpiece for the occasion and opened the conversation. 'Say buddie' – and, spotting his stripes, quickly changed tack. 'Mornin' sarge – we're British soldiers just arrived, we've bin told we can eat 'ere'. He looked up – I distinctly remember a gigantic number 1 on his uniform sleeve above his stripes and a couple of purple hearts, for wounds received. Draped over his shoulder was a lanyard and a sort of referee's whistle – a regimental honour.

'You Limeys?' he queried, looking us up and down through cigar smoke. 'Sure, sarge – just arrived and starving', I said, hoping the hint would get some action.

'Holy cow! Well, well', he drawled. 'Well fella, what would y'all like – anythin' for our allies. D'you guys mind eating off hash trays?' he said, pointing to a stack of segmented tin plates.

'No problem. Makes a change from our mess tins, 'eh fellas? It's the chow that counts.' We'd have eaten off the floor we were so hungry – we'd no objections to what our food came in, so long as it was clean. He called towards the kitchen 'Hey Freda. Fill these fellas' trays with essen, honey.'

We moved closer to see what the 'essen' was like. It was amazing: chicken, fries and sweetcorn, and a pudding, all on the same tray. We carried them over to our table – covered with a tablecloth – another luxury! Prospects improved still further when a nice looking fraulein poured out beer for us – she wore those long white socks and a cheeky grin that held promise.

There was silence for the next ten minutes or so, interrupted only by the sound of six chomping jaws. When we had finished the sergeant came over.

'Would you guys like some Hershey bars?'

There was confused silence. None of us knew what Hershey bars were, but the confusion didn't last long as he pulled a couple of chocolate bars out of his breast pocket. Confusion over – we nodded and grinned as he tossed the chocolate over onto our table. We sat back and relaxed with a smoke. This was the life! We dropped our ammo pouches and belts onto the floor, giving our bellies more room to sag into our khaki trousers. Some French troops appeared after a while wearing funny shaped hats, lanyards across their shoulders, the Cross of Lorraine on their sleeves and a sword and shield. Within seconds they were chatting up the cafe girls wholesale. We got up to go, telling the sarge to put the bill on the slate (which confused him a bit until we translated) and walked out feeling pleasantly full. The cafe was close to the main street of Zirndorf, within sight of the village square. Surrounding the square were a collection of shops, none of which with much to sell, and a cinema, which showed German and American films and was always full of off-duty military personnel. The Mayor's house and offices were further along the main road which led to the American and French camps. We spent an hour or so exploring the village and had a drink in the other cafe opposite the square before turning for home.

'Anyone fancy a walk in those woods?', said Jughead as we strolled back towards our billet.

'You crazy?! You don't know what's in there', I retorted.

'Well now's the time to find out', he said. 'Anyone comin' with me?'

'OK', said Bill, checking his service revolver, a Webley .45, which looked big enough to blow a bloody great hole through anything when fired. Walking through the trees we came across several bunkers. We had been warned of 'Wolf gangs' (armed renegades) roaming about the area and I was looking over my shoulder as I walked – straight into an underground bunker.

'Don't touch anythin'', Bill whispered, 'it might be booby-trapped!'

That didn't help my peace of mind. I could hear some machinery working – it must have been an ammo plant or something, right in the heart of the woods. Having scrambled out of the bunker and brushed myself down we walked on and soon came across an old guy dressed in a tattered overcoat, mittens which had seen better days and a German forage cap which had a small black and white disc inserted in it. There was fear in his face as we questioned him. He told us he lived in the woods and that other families lived there too, in the disused bunkers. Our German was just about non-existent so our questioning was limited; we offered him a cigarette which he accepted with alacrity, putting it carefully in his pocket. We returned to the house as dusk fell, discussing our finds in the woods and wondering what secrets the network of tunnels and the bunkers in there held.

For the next few days we were busy sorting ourselves out and getting settled in. We still ate our meals at the Cafe Bub, where the American sergeant saw that we were well provided for, but we managed to get a few other provisions like tea and sugar so that we could brew up when we wanted to.

Four houses along a ridge and two further ones over the brow of the hill from the village had been commandeered by the British. We were to be spread out in these houses, one of us at the Grand Hotel and one each at Stielen Strasse and Beethoven Strasse in the eastern suburbs of Nuremburg, about three miles from the centre. Freddie and I were detailed to look after a colonel and other officers as well as some civilian legal people at 'Lindenhof', a large house that had once belonged to a German brewer. Bill was in a small house next door. He was to look after a Captain Peter Casson and a Major Airey Neave when they arrived. Others were detailed to prepare the other commandeered houses. Two more blokes, both in the Coldstream Guards, had joined our party for this unusual set-up of military personnel and civilians banded under the title of the British War Crimes Executive, but it worked.

Jacko had been detailed for duty at the Grand Hotel. He was to look after the VIPs and others and, later, Captain Peter Casson who left Zirndorf to take over the public relations job at this large bombed one star hotel. Captain Casson occupied a suite on the first floor while he was in charge of PR for the Nuremburg Trials – his duties involved making the arrangements for the visiting guests and organising their evening entertainment, cabaret and floor shows in the Marble room. He attended to his duties like an ambassador. Like most of our officers he spoke fluent German; a likeable person with a dry sense of humour, I believe he was a Canadian.

Freddie and I moved into our billets and explored the house. There was a cellar with a big coal-fired boiler. The lounge held a baby grand piano and had french windows leading onto a terrace overlooking a large sweep of grass stretching to a fence on the boundary. On the first floor there were two bedrooms, a lavatory and a bathroom. We climbed yet more stairs to two more rooms, another lavatory and a large attic.

'I suppose this is our room, Fred', I said, as we stood in the attic.

'Yeah', he replied. 'Let's scrounge a couple of beds.'

'Where from?'

'Let's ask Bill next door and see how he's getting on.' We found Bill and asked him where he was sleeping. He showed us a room about the size of a cell, which looked cosy enough.

'Can we scrounge a couple of beds?', Fred asked.

'Sure', replied Bill, 'take as many as you want.'

'Very funny', I retorted. There wasn't a bed in sight, but after a search we found some in another house. With the beds in and one or two other bits and pieces, the attic became quite comfortable. I drew a buxom female figure in chalk on the slanting wooden ceiling over my corner bed and called her Blondie. She kept us company until I rubbed it off much later at the CO's request. Having settled our sleeping quarters, we could now concentrate on the job.

We had been detailed to recruit domestic staff to run the houses, about half a dozen of them, but this was posing a problem as our German was just about nil. We sat and smoked while we thought out ways and means and suddenly I had a brain wave.

'What we've got ter do is appoint a forelady who speaks a bit of English and who can select the staff from amongst the locals for us.'

'That's a clever move', said Bill, who had joined us, 'get someone who can do all the work and take the blame if anything goes wrong.'

'No, not really', I replied, realising that this really was the only way to organise the job. 'She would speak the lingo and knows better than us what staff is needed. She would know the local people better too. It shouldn't be hard to get staff. Have you seen the bloody bread queues? There's nothin' in the shops. That settles it then.'

We had another fag and relaxed on the long sofa in the lounge, knowing that we had solved a sticky problem.

'When d'you reckon the brass 'ats are arriving?' I asked Bill.

'Dunno', he replied as he stuffed more tobacco into his pipe. I gazed out across the garden and watched a seemingly endless stream of American army trucks droning by.

Time hung heavy during this period and we were often bored – a football would have helped to pass the time. We spent the days playing cards, using cigarettes for money. In those days cigarettes were real currency on both the black and open markets. In our cards games one fag was worth sixpence, but in the town the going rate was doubled.

Some of the lads spent hours writing to fiancées or wives. I was single and unattached, but I occasionally sent short notes to Mum and Dad. Our letters had to be handed in to the admin office at the Palace of Justice from where they were forwarded to their destination. It often took weeks to arrive and receiving mail from home was a rare luxury. Occasionally a package of local newspapers would arrive for me that had been nearly three months in transit. It was good to get these packages and to be able to while away a few hours reading about the old familiar places. Once or twice Ginger wrote – his lively descriptions of incidents, written in the vernacular, made me grin for hours afterwards.

Someone sometimes managed to get some beer and grub. It made a pleasant evening's pastime at the house. We even had music – our search of the house had unearthed a pile of 78 records. The only drawback was that they were the complete score of *Die Meistersinger* – in German. Not exactly to our taste, but it was music and it was all we had.

We normally ate at the Cafe Bub, but we didn't think much of American grub. They put bits of fruit in it – pineapple and things – and sweetcorn came with every meal. Chicken seemed to be the staple diet too, not that we minded that as much as the fruit and sweetcorn.

We collected food on the hash trays and exchanged the usual repartee with the buxom frau who served the grub. She had a limited vocabulary of American slang which she delivered in a heavy German accent, sounding just like Marlene Dietrich. 'Not so much of the "honey"', she retorted to my advances, as she spooned the fodder onto the tray.

'Dankershoon, baby', I replied with a grin, flashing one of my few German words at her. The big American sergeant who ran the place came over as we were picking over our meal. Out of the side of his mouth he hissed, 'Don't have much to do with that blonde, fellas she's a cocksucker.' We burst out laughing and stopped eating – looking over at her and then back at him.

'You've got ter be kiddin' Sarge!', I said.

'Nope, straight up fella, one of them goddamn Froggie guys was telling me. He caught them at it in the back.'

'Well I'll be blowed!'

'Have you tried her?'

'Nope, since I've got to work here it ain't easy pal!'

Fred and I were still laughing our heads off at this news.

'Fancy being served your food by a "gobbler"', I chortled. 'Fancy a sweet, Fred?'

'Do me a favour! I'm right off luxuries at the moment', he retorted, completely put off his food.

It didn't take long to find our forelady to look after things. She was a formidable woman, with black hair, piercing brown eyes and a back as straight as a ramrod. She told us she had lost her husband on the East front. I told her to recruit the staff we needed and that we would get the supplies required from Nuremburg.

Zirndorf was too small for any night life, so whenever we could we scrounged lifts into Nuremburg. I had got pally with a GI with the odd name of Irwin, who drove a jeep, and got lifts from him whenever possible. The jeep was nippy and it bounced over the roads as we sang our heads off.

One night we went into the city without Fred – he hadn't wanted to go. Irwin dumped the jeep in the compound near the railway station and we headed for the nearest beer keller. It didn't take us long to pick up a couple of young German girls and soon we were jammed into a corner of the Doughboys' night club with a huge pot of beer each for Irwin and me and glasses of Coca Cola for the girls. Those beer pots must have held nearly two pints each and the big frau serving us carried an incredible number of them in each hand. No wonder she had arms like a navvy's. The place was full, mostly with American military and any number of German girls. There was a small band playing and a German singer who sang like Lottie Lehmann and was accompanied by a pianist for her special number. The sequins on her dress glittered under the lights as she moved on the stage. Some of the guys wanted her to sing 'Lily Marlene' – a great favourite of the Africa Korps. Our conversation was limited to smiles and nods and the odd German word, although Irwin chatted away as usual, not just to his girl but to mine (called Renata) as well.

Every now and then the place was raided by the American MPs, who waded in and removed the drunks and any guys causing aggro, carting them off to the local slammer for the night – they were kept quite busy!

After dancing on the tiny dance floor to tunes like 'It Had to be You', 'Gonna Take a Sentimental Journey' and 'Where or When' Renata and I decided to split and said good-night to Irwin. I arranged to meet him at the jeep near the station later so that we could get back to Zirndorf before the curfew. It had got very misty but I wasn't bothered – I was too busy grabbing Renata round the waist as she led me to her flat. All I remembered of that walk was the old city wall with a steep drop on one side into a dry moat – I was too interested in Renata to notice where we were going. Eventually we arrived at her back door, and we made love there in the mist.

After we said goodnight I turned to make my way back to the central station and realised three things. I had no idea where I was, I had even less idea how to get back to the station and finally, it was well past curfew and Irwin would have left in the jeep. The mist had thickened considerably and I could only just see across the road. I was faced with a long walk back to Zirndorf after curfew, but at least the mist hid me from view. With a sigh I set off and soon came across what seemed a main road with tramlines in the middle – I knew that most trams went to the centre of the town so trusting I was going in the right direction I set off along this road. There wasn't a soul in sight – not surprising in view of the curfew – but despite my predicament I was on top of the world. I tried to walk quietly – fat chance in my hob-nailed boots and on cobble stones. At any minute I expected to be picked up by the Military Police. After what must have been about a quarter of an hour I saw a figure approaching out of the gloom. I reached inside my army tunic blouse for my pistol, a .32 automatic I had acquired some time before for self-protection – there were some pretty desperate people in Germany at that time. As the figure drew nearer I realised with relief that it was a GI or doughboy as we called them.

'Hiya Mac', he hollered, and I winced at the noise.

'Hi buddy', I replied in somewhat quieter voice. 'Say, d'you know if this is the right way for Zirndorf?'

'Search me, buddie', he replied cheerfully. 'I'm lost myself!' He stood there grinning, his teeth glowing white in the dark. He was slim, about

5ft 8ins, his sharp angular face topped by a forage cap tipped at an impossible angle over his left eye. On his hip he had a large revolver and his rubber soled boots made no sound as he walked. It emerged that he, too, had been seeing a girl home and was trying to leg it back to barracks without being spotted.

'Say, ain't you a Limey, fella?', he asked, after we had exchanged a few sentences.

'Sure, buddy', I replied. 'All the way from London Town, a Cockney – a superior kind of English.'

'No shit!' he said – 'I'm from New York, not far from Boston.'

'Well I've heard of it, Yank, but I can't say I know it.'

'Fancy meeting a John Bull here of all places – my grandfather told me about you John Bulls, you Briddishers and the rough times he had back in the old country.'

I was puzzled. 'Look, Yank, I don't know what yer talking about. What's yer name?'

'Flanagan.'

All became clear. He was of Irish descent. 'What's a nice Irish boy doing in the American Army?' I asked him jokingly. 'Look, what happened in the past is f... all to do with me – have a cigarette.'

'No – have one of mine', he said, pulling out a packet of Lucky Strike .

We stood there smoking and discussing the Irish Question – hours after curfew and with a south German mist swirling around in the darkness. Just two guys, miles from our homes, talking about the olden days against a backdrop of death and destruction. When we had finished the fags I slapped him on the back and reminded him that the Cockneys had arrived in the States long before his lot. Didn't the Mayflower leave from Rotherhithe docks (where she was built) with a Cockney captain and crew and wasn't the first baby born in Virginia from immigrants the child of a couple from St Bride's parish in the City of London? We said our goodbyes, the best of buddies.

'So long, Flanagan, take it easy pal – look out for your snowdrops.'

'Sure Mac – keep your eye on the tramlines, they turn left up there. Good luck John Bull.' He hollered back at me.

I hoped Fred had kept the door unlocked at the house. Some time later I found the river and left the faithful tramlines. At last I knew where I was. I turned into a country lane that led to Zirndorf and knew that I had about five miles to go. The only sound other than the grating crunch of my boots in the road was the sound of running water in the river. I had gone about a mile and it was still very foggy. I remember passing a copse when I heard a rustle coming from the trees. I suppose the noise from my boots had disturbed whoever or whatever it was.

As I reached for my pistol, shots rang out and bullets pinged and whined around me, hitting the farm wall behind me. I dived for the ground and returned fire with three quick shots in the direction of their firing point. I knew there were gangs of men operating in the area and I knew I was up against it. A fusillade of shots came desperately close – the only way to survive was to get over the farm wall in record time. I flung myself over and slipped down a grassy slope, landing in a heap on some rocks about 20ft below the wall and bashing my knee and leg on the way down. I lay there with my leg twisted under me expecting them to come after me and finish me off.

I had a couple of shots left and swore I was going to take two of the bastards with me. I was soaking wet and could feel blood from my leg soaking into my khaki trousers. A dog barked nearby – disturbed by the gunfire. I hardly dared move and lay there listening intently – the dog's barking must have woken the farmer and a glow of light shone from the farmhouse as I lay propped up against the boulder that had stopped me tumbling into the river. The guttural sounds of the farmer shouting – then telling the dog to shut up – must have frightened away my attackers, for I could hear twigs snapping and low voices getting fainter as they moved away. They must have believed that they had finished me off in the second bout of firing, and I wasn't inclined to point out their mistake. Indeed, it was all I could do to stay conscious, for I had also clouted my head hard on the way down. I lay there gripping my revolver and getting colder and colder as the swirling mist and icy water passed by my crumpled figure. By now, I was hurting like hell in several places.

I must have passed out, for the next thing I remember was waking suddenly in broad daylight. The mist had gone and now and then traffic rumbled by on the road above. I hollered for help, thanking my lucky stars I was still alive. No one heard my calls, which wasn't surprising, so I struggled to get upright and got my first aid kit from my hip pocket and tried to patch myself up. I was a hell of a mess – blood was caked over a large area of my trousers and they were stuck firmly to my leg. I couldn't stand on my left leg at all and realised that there was no way I was going to get back up the slope I had tumbled down. I started to crawl and drag myself along the river bank, hoping that before long the road would drop down to the level of the river. It was sheer hell on the boulders and cobbles but a lot easier on the grassy areas, which added bright green to my already multicoloured uniform – green, matted blood red and the original khaki were now highlighted by splashes and smears of slime, cow shit and God knows what else.

The road did eventually drop down to the level of the river and I was able to haul myself over the wall. After what seemed ages an American

Army truck appeared and rather than give him the traditional thumbs up sign for a lift, I stuck my arm out in the 'stop' sign. The driver sailed past me but changed his mind, skidded to a halt and reversed.

'Say buddie, you OK fella?', said the driver, jumping down from his cab and catching the full impact of my appearance.

'No. I'm not, mate', I replied, trying not to pass out again. 'Could you give me a lift to Zirndorf?'

'Well I guess so. My, you look all messed up, let's get a hold of you.'

I grabbed his shoulder thankfully and he dragged me towards the lorry, my left boot scraping along the gritty road, and somehow heaved me into the passenger's seat.

'Thanks, Yank', I said, as he climbed back into the driver's seat.

'I'm Jake', he said as we pulled away. 'We don't get many Limeys around these parts. You look in bad shape shape fella, what's been happening to yer?'

'I'm Boysie', I replied and told him the story.

'Those sons of bitches!', he exploded. 'Those chicken shittin' krauts. I thought we'd finished those Nazis off – killed 'em all off.'

'Looks like you missed some, Jake', I grinned, as he lit a Chesterfield from his pack and offered me one.

'There's an American Army hospital not far off. I'll drop you in to get patched up and then I'll report this incident back at base and they'll round those bastards up, no trouble. OK fella?'

'Thanks, Jake, you're a pal', I replied, and I meant it too.
He chatted all the way to the hospital. He told me he came from West Virginia and all about his home, wife and kids. Unlike Flanagan, he liked the British and thought 'that guy Churchill' was great.

We soon reached the hospital, much to my relief, for the pain was making me sweat. He half dragged and half carried me into the casualty department where he settled me in a chair and assured me that he would waste no time in getting a message to Fred at Lindenhof on his way back to Nuremburg.

Soon a nurse appeared and Jake saluted. 'One Limey delivered for repair, Ma'am', he announced. Turning to me, he winked. 'Take it easy, Limey. So long' and disappeared through the door. The nurse looked me up and down before saying anything. I must have presented quite a picture.

'OK soldier, would you mind getting your strides off behind that screen over there', she drawled, indicating a screen on the other side of the room. It was sheer hell getting 'over there'. Getting my trousers off, caked as they were with blood, and seemingly welded to my leg, proved too much for me. They had to cut them off. Eventually I was sitting, embarrassed, in my blood-stained underpants, having my leg swabbed by a female German orderly. The nurse came over as the job of cleaning me up was completed. She was a lieutenant, and even in my state I could appreciate her looks.

'My, that sure does look a mess', she commented. 'We'd better take a picture of that.' I was wheeled along and x-rayed, a blood sample taken, stitched up in several different places and tucked up in bed by the nurse, where I slept like a top for about 24 hours.

I spent several more days in the hospital and Fred came to see me and gave me all the latest gossip.

'Can't leave you alone for five minutes, Boysie, and see what happens when I do!', he joked in his homely Yorkshire accent.

I told him about Renata and we chatted about girl friends in general – he told me about a girl in Middlesbrough and how she didn't write regularly any more and what that probably meant. I told him about the ATS girl from Galashiels and how we had lost touch. In our situation, trying to maintain a steady relationship was well nigh impossible. We wondered what had happened to Irwin that night – he should have been alright – he had the wheels. When the conversation flagged we eyed the nurses and discussed their good points – they were all very tasty and Fred smacked his lips at them.

The day after Fred's visit the nurse and doctor came to see how my leg was doing and asked me to try walking around the ward. It felt terribly stiff but I managed to hobble to their satisfaction. They were pleased with the way the wounds were healing and after scribbling something indecipherable on my chart moved off, leaving me to the mercies of a Private First Class (PFC), who gave me an injection and bunged a thermometer down my throat to register my temperature. There was little finesse about his technique with the needle – he literally threw it into my arm and where it stuck, just like a dart, he pushed it home.

'Say, do yer ever miss, fella?'

'Sure sometimes when I hits the bone', he replied, unaware of the sarcasm in my question. 'Sometimes the guys in the line keel over and sometimes the goddam needle breaks in their arm.'

I almost asked him did he ever make double top but realised that the joke would be lost on him and didn't bother.

I asked for my uniform back when I was discharged. 'Sorry', was the reply, 'can't be done. We've had to burn it.'

'What! You've got to be kidding!'

'It was covered in blood and mess and we'd had to cut your trousers off – remember?'

I remembered then and asked them how I was going to get back, clad as I was in pyjamas.

'We can kit you out if you'll go down to the stores.'

A couple of GIs fitted me up with an American uniform and after trying several bits and pieces I stood there in gaberdine trousers, a shirt with a huge number 1 on it and a blouse tunic. The only wearable thing of my own were my trusty hobnailed boots. They didn't go as far as issuing me with their army pay book, much to my regret.

Fred turned up in a borrowed jeep to take me back to Zirndorf, and I said my goodbyes to the nurses and orderlies.

'What's bin happenin'?', I wanted to know as we drove away.

'Nothin' doing', replied Fred as we bowled along the road. 'Still looking for staff for the houses on the ridge.'

'How's Jughead?'

'OK.'

By now we had pulled into the Gymnasium which was occupied by transport staff. Fred handed back the jeep and we strolled slowly back up the hill to Lindenhof – me limping and wincing but getting there eventually.

'You look just like a Yank', joked Fred, as he strolled alongside me, looking me up and down. 'That figure 1 stands for the 1st Army doesn't it?'

'Yeah, bud and how do you like my accent?', I drawled.

'Waal hush my mouth with a rubber ball, honeychild', retorted Fred, repeating a comment we'd heard that became a standing joke with us. 'For a GI you sound like an Ukranian!'

Gradually our forelady built up a team of domestic staff to run the houses. There were plenty of people around needing employment, food and places to stay – the widespread devastation and invasions had left thousands of displaced people tramping through Europe, wandering around, pushing their belongings in battered prams, wanted by no one and with nowhere to go.

Civilisation had broken down to such an extent in Germany that normal values had disappeared, to be replaced by other values. Life was cheap and commodities replaced money. Cigarettes, soap and chocolate could get you anything. It sounds shocking now, but you could have a girl for two cigarettes and we made the most of our opportunities. The normal demographic pattern had been destroyed over much of Europe. Millions of young men had been killed or transported hundreds of miles away from their families, leaving a lonely and desperate female population struggling to stay alive and keep their children fed and clothed. The allied forces of occupation were a means of getting food or the currency to buy food – even if it meant sleeping with them. The needs of both were met – the allied soldiers were also missing normal relations, away from their own families. We made our own rules. I never slept with a married woman and I always used a condom. Some didn't bother and many a girl found herself pregnant.

More military staff arrived as time passed. A Royal Artillery sergeant moved into Jughead's house near the woods, while the Royal Army Service Corps (RASC) had taken over the Gymnasium with a few guys from the Tank Regiment, who were to act as extra drivers. It didn't take long for Harry, the sergeant and I to strike up a friendship and we spent much of our free time chatting up the frauleins and dating them whenever the opportunity arose. We soon lost count of the times we crept back to our beds in stockinged feet, our boots laced together and slung around our neck. We largely ignored both the curfew and the fraternisation rules and were lucky we weren't caught. As more and more squaddies arrived in the village and got into similar carryings on so the competition grew; but there were so many young widows as well as unattached girls around we never went short.

The thing that knocked our morale more than anything was boredom. The pace of activity hadn't built up yet. On one occasion one of the lads fired his bren gun at some rabbits in a field, hoping for rabbit stew instead of the interminable chicken at the Cafe Bub. The locals didn't appreciate the sound of the rat-tat-tat and complained.

Our leisure time was about to be curtailed, however, as a week or so later a 15 cwt army van drew up outside the house and out stepped a colonel and two majors. The colonel seemed to be in overall charge and moved into Lindenhof where Fred and I shared – we showed him over the house. He bagged the best bedroom in the place – the one with the french windows and the little balcony. The two majors, both of whom spoke fluent German, moved into the other bedrooms. Having settled in, the colonel sent for us. 'Well, McCarthy, I want you to look after me.'

I nodded my head, thinking to myself, 'What have I done to deserve this?' Of all the rotten luck. From now on I'd be under scrutiny, with very little time to myself. I caught Fred's eye – he was grinning all over his chops, thinking he'd escaped and knowing just what was going through my mind. The grin disappeared when the colonel told him he'd be taking care of the two majors. It was my turn to grin – two for the price of one!

Our domestic staff was now complete – our forelady had done her job well and the place was spick and span. A big tough-looking German bloke kept the boiler going and we always had hot water. Goodness knows where he got the fuel – I didn't notice any trees disappearing. Like so many Germans he'd seen action on the Russian front but he at least had returned – defeated but not dead or broken, which had been the fate of so many of them.

Slowly but surely the village and the houses filled up. Our attic was also taking shape. We had found an ironing board but couldn't get an iron anywhere. Our forelady suggested we asked at the burgermeister's office in the village. It seemed that if you wanted any kind of household gadget you applied for it at the burgermeister's office. Quite why, I never did work out. It seemed a good idea, so I rang the number and in my halting German explained what I wanted. What a palaver! You try explaining why you need an iron in German and see how far you get! Once I had broken the ice, and he had satisfied himself that we were the 'Tommies on the hill', he said he'd fix it for us. He'd send a fraulein up with one immediately. Fred's eyes lit up. Sure enough, a couple of hours later an iron was delivered.

We hung onto the record player and records too. I didn't understand the words but I thought the music was great, even though it drove Fred barmy.

Someone had managed to get hold of a football too, and we enjoyed playing football on the field in front of the house. Everyone joined in, even the German kids, and soon we had enough to make up teams and have proper competitive matches. It was a way of making friends in the village and getting some exercise.

As more and more officers arrived, so the transport system between Zirndorf and Nuremburg improved. We had had to rely on hitching lifts with the Americans or whoever else was going there. Some Humber Snipe cars appeared, driven by Welsh Guards who were based over at Stielen Strasse in Nuremburg. There was a variety of trucks and a couple of jeeps plus an old bus that was used at the start to ferry personnel to the Courthouse in Nuremburg, based at the Gymnasium, now occupied by our troops. There was even a sleek, shiny black bullet-proof limousine, obviously of American make, which fascinated us.

There was a red letter day when we each received an oval tin containing 50 De Reske Minor cigarettes – our rations for three months! At least they were free: I spent a happy few hours planning what I was going to spend my ration on.

It wasn't long before I had to teach the colonel the facts about cigarettes and finance in Germany. He wanted his shoes repaired.

'It will cost you, sir', I pointed out.

'How much?'

'Not money, sir, cigarettes.'

'Pardon?'

'Cigarettes sir. What d'you want doin' to them?'

'Just soled – the heels are OK.'

'That'll be about 20 fags' worth sir. He won't take money.'

'Preposterous! Where is this shop?', he demanded.

'Tucked away down behind some buildings in the village, sir.'

'Is he any good?'

'Yes, so I hear, sir. Anyway he's the only one and that's the going rate for the job.'

He looked at me quizzically and with a sigh got out a box of cigarettes and emptied it into the palm of my hand. He knew he was being conned and I had trouble keeping my face straight. 'How long will he take?', he demanded.

'Only a couple of days', I replied, as I busily counted the cigarettes.

I noticed they were a very nice pair of shoes as I carried them down to the village. I had only a vague idea where the place was. Hans the stoker had told me the address, and I eventually found the shop under an archway. I rang the bell and explained my errand to a pretty girl who answered the door. She showed me into a back room which was kitted out with shoe-mending gear – bits of leather, lasts, hammers, etc. The old cobbler was like something out of Hans Andersen or Grimm. An apron, grisled grey hair, steel-rimmed specs, I almost expected an elf in the corner. Through the girl, who had a smattering of English, I explained what I wanted and offered him ten fags. He shook his head. I offered him 15 fags and told him to take it or leave it. I said they were the Oberst's (Colonel's) shoes and I wanted my cut too! He accepted 15 cigarettes and promised the shoes would be ready in two days.

As I left I chatted his daughter up and asked her if she'd like to go to the kino, the local cinema, the next night as it was showing a German film. She told me that when the Americans came the rumour spread that they were the Tommies and they ran and hid – they came out again when they found out it was the Yanks.

On my way back I spotted a photographer's shop near the square and decided on the spur of the moment to have my picture taken. We argued the toss over the price and he finally settled for a few fags. I had tried to grow a moustache, Ronald Coleman style, but it was ginger and didn't really show, so there I was darkening it with a pencil (no good) and the heads of used matches (better). This carry-on amused the photographer no end. I took off my battledress blouse and sat in shirt sleeves holding a cigarette, trying to look nonchalant. The photo was a real success, well worth four fags.

I met the shoemaker's daughter, Trudi, the next day and spent a pleasant evening in the cinema and a better night making love in her bed. She was chubby and cuddly and warm and I made my usual dawn exit in socks so that I didn't wake up the old boy. It was my turn to make early morning tea, so I didn't bother going to bed. I mused on the girls I had slept with since I had arrived and decided that if it hadn't been me it would have been a Yank or a Free French as the latter called themselves.

We kept in touch with our mates who were, like us, organising the houses for the trial personnel. My old mate Jughead, for instance, was detailed to one of the houses scheduled for civilians. More and more arrived – the Gymnasium had beds set along its internal balcony, where the Tank Corps lads slept. I had struck up a friendship with one of them – another Londoner – who ran the football team and wanted me in it for a match against the French. The Royal Signals, meanwhile, had set up camp near the American base. I remember having a meal there once in a field kitchen, in mess tins as usual. It was only stew and rice pud, but never had basic Anglo Saxon food tasted so good after the interminable American fare. Mind you, we were grateful for some American goods – by now we were on PX rations, which meant we had a carton of cigarettes of our choice, like Lucky Strike, Camel or Chesterfields, plus five Hershey bars, all of which we bought at the Palace of Justice with our book of coupons. The store was so well stocked you could buy all the unobtainables!

It was in a field near Jughead's house that I unwittingly entertained a lorry load of GIs one afternoon. I had taken a German girl out for the afternoon and we had gone into a cornfield for a bit of slap and tickle. The trouble was that the corn had just been harvested and we were trying to make love on the stubble – talk about a bed of nails! I put my jacket under her but she wiggled and complained – the stubble was sticking into her bottom – it was murder for me too, as the stuff pierced my knees and thighs. Try as hard as I could it was no good – we just couldn't concentrate and eventually gave it up as a bad job. I stood up and was just pulling my pants up when a chorus of hoots, whistles, cheers and clapping came from the other side of the hedge. They had hugely enjoyed the entertainment! I shrugged my shoulders and arms, and called over to them. 'Do me a favour guys.' I could well do without an audience.

The free and easy life at Zirndorf came to an end when I received orders to report to Nuremburg, where I was to take over number 16 Stielen Strasse and get it ready for Lord Justice Lawrence, one of the judges at the trial.

7

Nuremburg

I managed to hitch a lift into Nuremburg and sat in the front seat of a jeep alongside a very tall good-looking GI who was going as far as the Grand Hotel just by the railway station. Chatting to him and taking in the passing scenery as we drove through the countryside, he told me he was from Georgia and had received a 'Dear John' letter from his fi-ancée back home. There was nothing he could do about it. I tried to console him with the old saying 'There's more pebbles on the beach, mate' – he just laughed. We passed the courthouse where the trials were about to begin. American tanks, armed jeeps with mounted ma-chine guns and lorries with backup troops surrounded the place. We passed through a couple of check-points – only the trams were waved through – and arrived at the hotel. I thanked my country cousin Hank for the lift and wished him well. 'Take it easy fella and good luck with the next bird.' He pushed his cap to the back of his head and drove off.

I still had to get down to Stielen Strasse which was a turning off the main road and too far to walk. I popped in to see Jacko, explained the problem to him and as quick as a flash he had a car waiting outside the hotel for me. Sitting in the car I could see queues everywhere and crowds of displaced people wandering dejectedly around. Very few buildings remained undamaged. Most of the city had been virtually destroyed and the parts that hadn't were being taken over for the trials. People rummaged amongst debris trying to salvage anything of value. Even the Grand Hotel was far from grand, decorated by scaffold-ing towards the rear of the building as the American Army Engineers busily repaired the badly damaged structure. The hotel accommodated a good many of the American personnel who worked at the trials.

We couldn't find Stielen Strasse amongst the rubble that littered the very long devastated road. 'Hold on a minute – I'll nip out and ask for directions from that old man', I said. My German was improving to the point where I could do this and understand the reply. I had begun to wonder whether the house still stood as we had moved past street after street that had been destroyed. But eventually, by following the old man's instructions, we found Stielen Strasse and pulled up outside number 16. It was an imposing house with large windows. I knocked on the door and got no reply at first, but finally I roused the housekeeper in the basement, a nice looking woman who, on recognising my uniform, waved me in. A chap of her age was in the room – she introduced him as 'her man' – and we shook hands. She called a name and a smashing looking young girl of about my age came in – this was Rosie, their daughter. Rosie spoke English and was beautiful – she had black curly hair and rosy cheeks and a beautiful smile. I told her that I was there to get the house ready for an important visitor.

'Ja, I know', she replied, 'I will show you the house.'

It was a lovely house, with an imposing hallway and staircase. I particularly remember the master bedroom as it had a beautiful painting above the bed which really took my fancy. At the top of the house was a large attic and a small room adjoining which I bagged as my bedroom. The house was kept spotless by Rosie's mother, the floors always highly polished, and hell to walk on in hobnailed boots, especially when you were trying not to make a noise. There were two houseboys, Hans and Fritz.

At the back of the house was a conservatory in which was a piano and a gramophone. As we got to know each other we used to dance in the conservatory in the evening, as Rosie tried to teach me the Viennese Waltz. Hans and Fritz would join in and dance together in a stiff matter-of-fact fashion. These nice little socials didn't last long, though. One evening we were whirling round to the music of Strauss when in walked several officers. They stopped in the doorway and we stopped in our tracks. I turned the gramophone off and the two German lads disappeared silently. I was left with Rosie on one side and the officers on the other – one slapping his boots with his cane. I explained that I was having dancing lessons and quickly offered to escort them round the house – anything to break the silence and embarrassment. They obviously disapproved strongly of fraternisation and made it very clear that it was to stop – as innocent as it was. The tour of inspection finished, we discussed food arrangements and catering. I told them that I got the food from the Grand Hotel and that the hausfrau cooked it on the premises. 'Her man' was responsible for the hot water, he being the stoker.

Soon after a few Welsh Guards arrived and bunked down in the attic. The house was beginning to fill up.

I visited the Grand Hotel regularly for food supplies. The Americans had all the food flown in from the States by their Air Force and stored it in the cellars of the Grand Hotel, despatching deliveries from there to all their eating places and camps. The store was run by an American, Colonel McCormick, who always saw I was OK for stuff. Jacko was based there and I used to drop in for a chat, using the dusty back stairs.

One day I had to go to the British Delegation office in room 239 to be photographed for a pass in order to get in and out of the Palace of Justice, where the International Military Tribunal was about to begin. I was officially part of the British War Crimes Executive apparently – what a title for someone who looked more like a GI (I was still wearing the clothes they gave me in hospital). I had my picture taken whilst I held a small blackboard with my name in chalk on it and was given the pass number of 1355 to satisfy the guards who stopped you every 20 yards or so inside the building.

'O.K. fella, you're doing fine.' The 'snowdrop' (an American sentry with white helmet) muttered as I presented the pass to him for the first time.

One afternoon we finally heard that our VIP would be arriving, so there was great bustle and hustle preparing the house and lighting fires to air the rooms. I gave the house the final checkout and the next day Lord Justice Lawrence arrived to take up residence. His wife came over a few days later, although wives had been banned. The French judges came with theirs, however, and others quickly followed. Lawrence was, I believe, to be the President of the Judges at the Military Tribunal.

We came face to face in the bathroom of all places – I was checking that all was OK when he walked in. He was small and I towered over him as he stood there in a very sober looking suit, squat, round-faced and almost bald, but with an eagle eye which at that moment was gazing at a decanter full of water.

'Is that water treated?' he queried.

'Yes sir', I replied. He nodded and walked back to the bedroom – the one with the oil painting above the bed, the painting I would have loved to have owned myself. The minute his back was turned I popped a water purifying tablet into the decanter and left the tin on the shelf. I could understand his caution: there were so many damaged water mains, and so many corpses still lying rotting in the piles of debris and in the streams. You had to suppress the smell with a handkerchief over your face if you got near. I just hoped he didn't want a drink until the now cloudy water had become clear again.

Rosie's mother was a good cook and I managed one way or another to keep the Lawrences well fed – even when what was available was limited. Transport between the house and the Palace of Justice consisted of a battered jeep, pretty basic. Lawrence sat in the back with his briefcase, books and a bowler hat, while a pal of mine, a sergeant in the redcaps, sat up front, holding a Sten light machine gun, next to a Welsh Guardsman driver.

Soon after the Lawrences arrived, I was transferred again and told to report to a much smaller and more homely house in Beethoven Strasse to replace a bloke on leave. Sir Norman Birkett and his wife 'Billy' lived here. He was a complete contrast to Lord Justice Lawrence, very tall and slim, sandy haired and bespectacled. He walked with a stoop, his angled face and his long straight nose giving him the look of an eagle. In the 1930s he had been involved in two of Britain's most famous murder trials – Dr Buck Ruxton and the Brighton trunk murders. His wife often wore check lumberjacked styled blouses and I got it fixed in my head that she was a Canadian. They were a lovely couple and as they were in the habit of holding dinner parties, I was often asked to ensure that there was enough food. On one occasion 'Sandy' (as Sir Norman was called) asked if I would serve at the table as he was giving a dinner for some of the top Russian, French and American legal personnel. I didn't mind – having worked as a waiter at Lyons Corner House I knew what to do. I told him we had some canned chicken, which pleased him. He wanted me in military uniform, as that would please the Russians. The meal was a success. I served the wine in my best Guards uniform, shining like a new pin, while the women served the food, dressed in black and lace. I stood at the back of the room until the meal was finished.

I had promised one of the maids to escort her home afterwards, but it turned out to be some distance away, and all I had with me was my tribunal pass with photo – I left my trusty .32 at home. We walked arm in arm for a long way, through the American Army camp, and eventually arrived at a block of flats. I was invited in for a drink – an offer I would normally have accepted with alacrity, but it had been a long day and I said goodnight after a quick kiss and cudddle. I lit a fag and started to walk home back to Beethoven Strasse. I got through the well-lit Army camp alright and struck out along a track which followed the crest of a ridge – it was a lovely night and I remember I could see the stars twinkling and was just thinking how peaceful it was when suddenly the sound of gunfire close by shattered the peace.

I stopped dead, wondering what the hell was going on. I could see lights and could dimly make out a line of troops coming up the hill towards me. A flare lit up the scene in an eerie green light as a hail of bullets whistled towards me. I looked down the slope, not believing what was happening.

'Bloody hell', I said to myself, as the grim reality of the situation hit me like a thunderbolt. 'They're firing at ME.'

I froze as they charged towards me. The bullets pinged and whined around me – how the hell they missed me I shall never know, but obviously my name and number weren't on any of them. The soldiers reached me and I was surrounded by a ring of bayonets and tommy-guns. Worse still they were speaking in a completely unrecognisable language. What appeared to be an officer approached me, pistol in hand. Believe me, I thought my last moment had come. He said something to me but I couldn't understand him. 'I am an English soldier', I told him but he didn't understand me any more than I understood him. I couldn't imagine who they were, although in retrospect I think they must have been Russians. I slowly reached my breast pocket in which I had my pass with my photograph and identity, but in the circumstances I don't think it would have made any difference. I showed him my pass but in the gloom he couldn't read it, and he didn't understand what it said anyway. I tried German and a few French phrases as well as a couple of Italian words, even GI slang. I was getting mad now, but none of them responded to anything I said. In desperation I pointed to my shoulder flashes which said 'Grenadier Guards.' Still nothing. All the time I expected one in the back – I was still completely surrounded and they looked pretty grim. It was stalemate. The leader looked again at my pass and hesitated and then a miracle. He half saluted and handed my pass back, murmuring some unintelligible words as he did so. I stood stock still fearing that if I moved one of them would shoot – no messing! The tension eased and I lit a fag as the mystery platoon melted away in the gloom. I faced them blowing cigarette smoke in their direction – I didn't want them to use my back as target practice – and then I made for home.

Later the next day I heard that some prisoners had escaped from a camp in the area – I assumed that's who they had been looking for. To this day I still haven't a clue who they were and can only guess that they were Russians although I never saw the red star in their caps.

I crept upstairs to bed – and I never slept a wink. 'Who were they? What were they doing in Uncle Sam's territory?' I wanted to know. I never did get any answers. Thank God they were lousy shots.

It was good to get back to the security of everyday routine among people with whom I could communicate the next day. I used to scrounge a lift into the Grand Hotel with Sir Norman to save on fuel and transport. We used the jeep, the redcap in front holding a tommygun alongside the driver, whilst I sat at the back with Sir Norman. That day, I presented my shopping list with a salute to Colonel McCormick, and made damn sure I got on well with him. It paid to cultivate people in key positions and to salute. I was never sure whom to salute in the American Army – they had so much 'fruit and scrambled egg', as well as lanyards, etc., that I always gave them the benefit of the doubt. Colonel McCormick's word was law at the Grand Hotel.

I showed him my list and he read it carefully, ticking off the products before bawling out 'Malone – see to this fella – and make sure he gets everything on that damn list.'

'Yessir', replied Malone, hurrying to do as he was told.

The colonel's face didn't crack, but he winked at me before turning on his heels and striding off to terrorise another part of the hotel. I returned to the jeep and chatted to my redcap mate – a huge red-faced bloke – while we waited for Sir Norman.

' 'Ave you been in and watched the trials yet, Mac?', he wanted to know. I replied that I hadn't, not yet.

'You want to, you know', he replied. 'It's not every day you'll see a show as good as this one.'

I decided to go the next day. I wasn't exactly in the mood for wandering around yet anyway, after the experience of the night before.

Early next morning we set sail again – Evans the driver, my redcap mate and Sir Norman and I in the back – me taking it all in and feeling much better after a good night's sleep.

At the main entrance there were two GIs on sentry duty wearing white helmets, gloves, etc. They faced inwards – looking at each other – not forward as is more usual. I walked past them and showed my ID card to the guard.

'OK fella', he said, as I brushed past his small desk in the corridor. Every 20 yards or so we went through the same procedure varied only by different catch phrases. After a series of these encounters I eventually arrived at the foot of the stairs. It was security gone bonkers, typical American overkill – these guys took no prisoners! I looked around. It was a marvellous building with marble floors and walls and high ornate ceilings. I wondered what to expect as I climbed the stairs. Men and women in a variety of uniforms bustled to and fro looking very important or harassed. I had to show my pass yet again and eventually I pushed open a double door which revealed a balcony, like the dress circle in a theatre, with tip up seats. It was early and there were only a few people there so I chose a seat in the front row and played around with the headphones while I waited for the action to start. You moved a switch, according to the language you wanted. The huge hall gradually filled up and by the time the proceedings were ready to begin the place was packed.

Below me were the main objects of most people's interest – the Nazi leaders. They sat in a long pew, as if they were in church. I stared at them and remember thinking how yellow and gaunt they looked sitting there, as if they were suffering from yellow jaundice – could it have been the lights? Some were in uniform, others were dressed in a variety of outfits. Behind them stood the 'snowdrops', the GI guards wearing white helmets; in front were their defence lawyers and barristers. Some Nazi leaders, like Goering, defended themselves. Across the floor on a raised bench were what I presumed to be the prosecuting counsel and the judges. I recognised Lord Justice Lawrence and Sir Norman Birkett. The two French judges were dressed in lace and frills as well as black gowns. The Russian judges were the only ones in military uniform.

I couldn't help thinking at the time that surely, if this was a Military Tribunal, everyone sitting in judgement should have been in military uniform. It seemed that for once only the Russians were correctly dressed. What were those civilians doing, judging in a military court? The Russians wanted all the defendants dead – nothing else would satisfy them – and although they went along with the trial, they were obstinate and obstructive, much to the chagrin of everyone else.

Proceedings took so long that it soon became boring and repetitive. During one particularly deadly session, my mind wandered and I began to consider how much right each of the nations sitting in judgement there had to try these men. The Russians were guilty of atrocities every bit as bad – Katyn Forest in Poland just one example. The British too had been guilty of bombing Dresden in just the same way as the Germans had bombed Coventry. The Americans had dropped the atom bomb on Hiroshima. The Vichy police had committed atrocities on their own people in France. No one was innocent, whatever the excuses. This train of thought made me uneasy, so I reached for my headphones and switched on to Sir Hartley Shawcross.

The translators and the press corps sat at the far side of the court. Behind the judges' bench panelled windows overlooked the floor, marking the small rooms used by newsreel crews and broadcasters for radio stations throughout the world. In one of these rooms sat the official war artist Dame Laura Knight, who painted the scene set below for the War Office.

When the sun shone, dust-laden shafts of light lit the room, giving it a cathedral like quality. Some of the prisoners seemed to doze through the proceedings, but the corpulent figure of Goering was full of life, as he watched every move and took everything in as the others stared blankly into space or nodded with sleep. All the big names were there except for Martin Bormann, who was missing, and Ley, who had committed suicide. These were early days yet and each side seemed to be sparring. The real action would come later and I promised myself I would be there.

At the back entrance of the Grand Hotel, where yet again I showed my pass, I climbed the dusty back stairs in hope of seeing Jacko. He was catching up with some shut-eye when I knocked, and his bleary eyes struggled to focus on me as he answered the door.

As he poured us a drink he wanted to know how much I made on a carton of American cigarettes. I told him that in Zirndorf I got 200 marks. He laughed like a drain when he heard this, delighted to have scored off me for once. 'I get 400 here', he crowed, grinning from ear to ear. That was about £10 profit for 200 cigarettes – a lot of money in those days.

'You sly old son of a bitch', I shouted at him. 'Then I'd better do my tradin' down 'ere in future. What d'you get for soap and chocolate?' All these commodities were widely used as cash, especially on the black market.

We exchanged gossip and news over a drink and a fag. He was in charge of the VIPs in the hotel who had come for the trials. He looked after them and got whatever they wanted from wherever he could get it – a job that required all the initiative he had. He was a shrewd operator and well suited to the job. The job suited him too – he had the pick of the maids and the place was full of American women, most of them officers, all of them fair game as far as Jacko was concerned. Like a kid in a sweet shop, he was. Financially he was OK too, between his wheeler dealings and big tips from guests for services rendered.

'Do you fancy some chow?' he asked.

'Where?', I wanted to know.

'Just follow me – I eat with the GIs in the canteen they've fixed up in the basement, good place for a nosh and plenty of it, too.'

'OK whiz-kid, lead the way.'

I told him about my adventures of the night before last and how that had almost been my last kiss and cuddle. After sausage and french fries, especially cooked for us by one of his girl friends, I had to take my leave of Jacko. It was time to get back to duty. I left and, as luck would have it, ran smack into Lewis, one of the drivers.

'Eh boyo, what you doin' 'ere?', he grinned. He had just delivered yet another VIP and carried his luggage up for him.

'Say, Taffy – you going back?' I put my arm round his shoulder. 'Gis a lift.'

'Sure kiddo', he replied, opening a packet of Woodbines and offering me one as we strolled back to the car. There I was, puffing away at my Woodbine in the luxury of the back seat of the Humber Snipe staff car. I was dropped off at the house, where I chatted with the GI sentry at the gate before I went back on duty. Like most he was pissed off, homesick and bored and our chats helped to pass the time, especially at night when I came creeping in out of the gloom – often scaring the pants off them. The names I got called by them would make a trooper blush! In contrast the female military staff were having a ball, as the escorts vied for their company.

Christmas was approaching and there were parties, some unofficial get togethers and others official, like the one that the United Nations

Relief and Rehabilitation Administration (UNRRHA) put on. The UNR-
RHA's purpose was to give aid to refugees and people of occupied
countries, mainly in Germany. This big get together was a very large
affair, and we had all been invited. The party was great, but I got plastered and had to be driven home and helped up to bed, missing half
the fun.

Soon I was back at Lindenhof again, in the attic with Freddie and it
was good to be back. By now there were two civilians as well as the
colonel and the majors in the house – one was Elwyn Jones, a barris-
ter. Bill next door was now looking after Captain Peter Casson and Major Airey Neave. Other personnel were in other houses in the village.
Lt. Col. Mervyn Griffith-Jones, Sir Hartley Shawcross, Sir David Maxwell-Fyffe, G.D. (Khaki) Roberts, Colonel Phillimore and Captain Barrington were all billeted in Zirndorf.

After some hard negotiations with Freddie, I took responsibility for
the majors and the civilian. We had acquired a male chef and his tan-
trums, as well as extra kitchen staff. All the officers were having their
meals at Lindenhof in the lounge and I noticed a large barrel of beer
on tap, a fact I duly noted and took advantage of whenever the opportunity presented itself.

I stowed my stuff away in the attic and went downstairs. I found the
major's Sam Browne hanging in the wardrobe, looking decidedly in
need of attention. I took it back upstairs and showed it to Freddie.
'Looks as if it hadn't seen polish in a month of Sundays', he commented as I rummaged around for polishing gear.

'Well 'ere goes', I said. 'This is going ter be the smartest officer's belt
in the business. 'e'll be able to shave 'imself in it by the time I've finished.' I set to – but it was a long time before I was happy with it. Later, when the major went home on leave, the colonel took a good look
at the Sam Browne as he said goodbye and congratulated Neave on its
appearance. That gave me a lot of satisfaction, although nothing was
said to me!

It wasn't long before I re-established trade with my Zirndorf contacts, notably the stoker who kept our boiler going. I had to tell him
the price of fags had gone up. I sold or traded anything I could lay my
hands on – sometimes I even set up a small stall – and my savings
grew nicely. I discovered Hans the stoker had been reselling his cigarettes at a much higher price, so I began taking them into Nuremburg
and making the extra profit myself.

Christmas was only days away as I looked out of the window and
wondered if the old bus had arrived – it took our personnel to the Nuremburg court each day from a couple of pick-up points. The hard
seats and the rough roads made it an uncomfortable journey. As I

watched I saw a staff car pull up and four officers get in, so I presumed that things were looking up and that the old bus had finally been abandoned.

There was to be a party at the gymnasium for all ranks, paid for by the officers and legal men before they went on leave. The highlight of the evening was a challenge between Sir Hartley Shawcross and Sir David Maxwell-Fyffe to see who could be the first to climb to the top of the ropes in the hall of the gymnasium. There was general cheering and banter and taking of sides – there were even bets taken. We all pressed forward and formed a tightly packed group around the two.

Up they both started but first one then the other slipped back to the ground. Two of the best legal brains in the country dangling there like a pair of school boys, yelled on by a crowd of drunken squaddies! Finally Sir Hartley got his act together and began to climb again, but so did Sir David – one slipped a little and a roar went up. They were almost there – they had to touch metal at the top – but Sir David put in a late challenge. Too late. Sir Hartley touched first and a great cheer went up, but it was a close run thing. It ended with a handshake.

At the end of the evening we staggered out to a frosty, starlit night and meandered and skidded up the slippery slopes to our beds.

Harry had got to know a couple of Polish girls while I had been in Nuremburg, so one free afternoon he suggested we go and see them. I smarmed my hair down with some American hair cream I had managed to get and we set off.

'Where we goin, 'Arry?', I wanted to know.

'It's on the outskirts of the village', he replied

'What's my bird like?'

'So so.'

' 'Ow d'you meet them?'

'They came lookin' for work.'

'Oh yeah! Tell me more.'

'Not far now, Boysie', said Harry, as we plodded through the fields.

'But 'Arry, there's no 'ouses 'ere.'

'It ain't an 'ouse it's a camp.'

'A camp? What d'you mean a camp?'

'A displaced person's camp, a refugee camp, got it?'

'You've got ter be kiddin, 'Arry.'

'Nah, straight up', he replied. 'Them's a couple of beauties.'

'I'll take your word for it.'

By now we were standing by a fenced-in field covered with wooden shacks. We'd not been there long when two gorgeous blondes came out. One had flaxen plaits tied with ribbon, the other wore a beret at a saucy angle – like those French adagio dancers. Introductions were soon over and I really took a shine to this particular blind date. 'You're right, Harry', I hissed as we moved off. 'A pair of real smashers.' We walked along the river bank, tossing stones in the water, laughing and indulging in mild horseplay, then we were invited back to their shack. I looked over to Harry to see his reaction. All he did was tilt his head on one side and put his hands out as if to say 'Why not?' I followed his lead – after all he was the sergeant. Not that I needed much persuading.

It was getting dark as we reached the hut and as we walked through the door the smell hit me. Looking round the large room I noticed the central wood-fired stove with its flue going out through the ceiling. A line of old clothes reached from one wall to the other – a makeshift curtain which gave elementary privacy for three families and any number of the kids for whom this hut was home. Mums and Dads sat round the stove and there was a stack of wood to keep the stove going.

They looked up and smiled at us as we walked in, chattering to the girls in Polish. One of them had a little English and translated. They had lost everything and now were forced to live in appalling conditions, unwelcome in this new country yet unable to return to Poland. The only furniture seemed to be a couple of large beds in the corners and whatever they were sitting on. With our halting German and their limited English we managed short bursts of conversation, but it was hard going.

It was getting late so I made ready to leave, but the old people were making us a drink so the girls pressed us to stay the night. We agreed. I certainly didn't want a night time walk again after the last incident.

'Where we kipping, 'Arry?' I whispered, looking round the joint.

'Over there', he replied, nodding towards one of the beds. So the four of us shared a large bed while the old people sat round the hot stove chatting about old times, taking no notice of us – just nodding and smiling, knowing bloody well what was going on. Somehow I didn't fancy the place or the bed – I knew too much about livestock in overcrowded places from my days in the Bunk, but I pushed such thoughts away and climbed over quite a few bodies before I reached the wall where my date was lying giggling.

As we staggered back to our duties early next morning, walking over the railway level crossing, Harry started scratching. I kept my distance, saying that we'd better have a quick bath as soon as we got in – just in case.

Christmas Eve arrived complete with heavy snow. Fred and I invited our mates round for a few drinks as we had managed to get some booze. The trials at the Palace of Justice had adjourned for the holidays and most of our legal staff had gone home. The prisoners, on the other hand, were spending their Christmas locked in cells under the building, guarded night and day by po-faced 'snowdrops.' It was debatable who were more bored – the prisoners, who must have been relieved not to have to sit through the interminable trials, or the 'snowdrops.'

The lads left us with empty bottles and made a hole in the beer-barrel that stood in the officers' mess, and they took the two maids as well, so we relaxed on our bunks playing records and smoking. The snow was falling very fast and just before midnight the bells of the little Catholic Church across the road began to ring out. We went to the window and looked out.

'Good grief, look at that', said Fred as we caught sight of the silent crowds converging on the candlelit church.

'It must be Midnight Mass', I said. 'D'you reckon they'd like to hear our record of Silent Night?'

'Dunno, we could give it a try.'

So we wound up the record player and placed it on the window sill after brushing off the snow. We played 'Stille Nacht' by a Nuremburg choir and the crowd outside looked up, wondering where the heavenly choir was coming from. They probably thought we were cranks, but it was our gesture of goodwill.

Bill came round from next door and asked if we wanted to go to church the next day.

'Yeah sure', we replied, 'but where's the Protestant church?'

He knew that there was one near the American barracks so we arranged to meet and go there.

The night became very cold and it was definitely sub zero in our attic, so we piled our greatcoats on our beds to try to keep warm. The officers had promised us tea in bed on Christmas morning and colonel and the majors were doing the honours, so we had that to look forward to. We were awoken by a clattering on the stairs as the officers brought two mugs of steaming hot tea, but we pretended to be asleep, which was a mistake. They simply pulled the bedclothes off us, not funny in the freezing temperatures. We 'woke up' sharpish and returned their Christmas greetings and exchanged the usual barrack room banter. After breakfast we went over to the American garrison church and sat towards the back. The place was full of GIs and servicewomen and the Pastor was one of the officers. In contrast to the south German Catholic churches it was very plain inside, austere almost, but the place was made festive by masses of flowers. Where they had come from I don't know, for there was nothing growing outside. I suppose they must have been flown in from the States. As we sat there listening to the sermon, I was fascinated as much by the Pastor's long, drawling accent as by the content of his talk. After the service we lined up to shake his hand. I thanked him for a lovely service and he said how nice it was to have 'three Briddishers' in his congregation. We returned to the house feeling good inside and later enjoyed an enormous Christmas dinner at the Cafe Bub in the village. It wasn't the traditional British fare – and there was the inevitable sweetcorn.

'No sweetcorn, sarge', I said quickly as he aimed a huge spoonful at my mess tray.

'You know, fella', he replied, 'I can't stand the stuff myself the way it's cooked here; I like it on the cob.'

'How about filling the gap with french fries, Sarge?'

'No french fries, but I tell you what, pal, I'll give you a double ice cream.'

'Yeah? Do me a favour! There's five feet of snow outside! Just bung the cranberry sauce on the plate, brother.'

The place was decorated with holly and ivy and a sprig of mistletoe that hung over the counter, and I smiled as I looked up to it. We tucked in and really enjoyed our meal. We always did well there for food – ham and eggs for breakfast and chicken most days for dinner, but it was always coffee to drink and fruit in the meal that spoilt it. Our brew ups at the house were almost a religious ritual, as it was just about the only time we drank our beloved tea.

On New Year's Eve there was a dance in the village hall, so Bill, Fred and I went – only to find the place packed out with French and American soldiers who had got there first and bagged all the birds. We sat drinking from the enormous steins which had been brought to our table by a mountainous German woman. She carried five of these huge pots in each hand with no effort at all, and her saucy grin got us going as she plonked three of the pots on our table – 'Prima sweetheart, just prima' I said, giving her a tip of a couple of fags. The three of us were cheesed off. Fred decided to go and spend the evening with his girl back at the house. She worked as a servant there, and ever since Fred clapped eyes on her, he'd been smitten. He was determined to marry her, despite the very real problems. Bill and I sat there a while longer as the place and the bar got more and more crowded. The German band was playing its heart out to the accompaniment of singing frauleins and the beer was flowing – much of it on to the floor, as dancers jostled the waitresses. It was like trying to dance in the tube at rush hour. Some GIs were messing around and twirling their shrieking partners round very fast in a Viennese waltz; one pair overbalanced and knocked into a pair of French soldiers at the bar who were plastered. They ended up on the floor. The next thing was a general punch up between the French and the GIs and general panic among the German girls.

Bill and I slipped out of a fire escape door as a jeep full of Military Police poured in the front door to hoik out the drunks and chuck them in the stockade until they were sober.

Down at the Gymnasium the festivities were going with a swing and we soon got into the mood. The only problem there was a shortage of girls. I ran into Johnny, a pal of mine who ran the football team and we chatted for a while. He had managed to find a couple of ex-pro footballers – one from Celtic and one from Rangers, both now in the Scots Guards – and he'd also got some talented Taffys.

'I want you for the left wing, Spiv', he said. 'We've got the makings of a bloody good team, and I've got a match fixed up with the Frenchies. What d'yer say?'

'But I've got no boots, mate', I replied.

'Play in plimsolls then.'

'Yeah yeah in this snow 'n' ice – you gotta be joking pal!'

We eventually agreed that when the weather improved I'd play in his team. The discussion then turned to the shortage of 'crumpet', which had become increasingly acute as more and more military arrived. Someone came up with the idea of picking them up from Nuremburg station.

'Why there?', someone asked.

'Because that's where they go if they've got nowhere ter stay or if they are waiting for a train.'

'Why not give it a try? You've got nothing ter lose except your virginity!', said one bloke, slinging his cap in the air.

'All we need is a three tonner with flaps at the back, one driver and two to chat them up.'

'Is it agreed then?'

'Yeah' came the chorus.

A roster was drawn up and I was chosen as one of the two to do the pick up. I was to do the talking, the other mate from the Tank Corps to be the driver. The plan was to drive over at about 7p.m. and offer bed and breakfast and fags plus transport back to the station in time for their trains. We put the plan into operation the next night and I mentally rehearsed my patter in German as we drove in. The station platforms were packed with people stranded in transit. It wasn't easy to approach the young girls together, but as the temperature dropped below zero our task got steadily easier. We got five fags for each girl we delivered and ten if the squaddies were older! I was going to be quite well off. We soon had about 15 or 16 giggling girls in the back of the lorry.

Back at the Gymnasium the girls were soon paired off – there were some smashers amongst them and the blokes who wanted them had to cough up ten fags. We did well that night. Soon there were giggles and grunts from the beds up on the balcony. At least they were warm that night – and we made sure they got a good breakfast the next morning before dropping them off back to the station. There were no complaints. One or two girls had been a bit alarmed at first but had relaxed with a hot drink and food and the friendly atmosphere.

I nicknamed the nightly lorry run the 'Bahnhof Express'. The name stuck.

With the New Year over we were back to usual routine. There was an urgent call for all British personnel to report to the court house. Something big had cropped up at the trial and more paper evidence was needed in a hurry. We went from Zirndorf en bloc and eventually made it to room 239 after showing our passes to a series of 'snowdrops'. Someone was there already barking orders to us as we came through the doors. The duplicators were in full swing and we were soon hard at work collating, checking and stacking neat bundles. There was a mountain of paper piled in the BWCE room by the time we had finished. We took short breaks when we could.

On the second day I was out of the room for a quick fag when I saw a vision down the corridor. An extremely beautiful woman was striding down the marble-floored corridor, her high-heeled shoes clicking on the floor and echoing round the walls as she walked. I gazed at her through the cigarette smoke, her long black hair tied back and swinging as she walked and moved her head. She had a fresh complexion and wore a white blouse and straight black skirt. Scurrying alongside her were a couple of men and as she talked to them her white hands moved expressively – like Pavlova doing the dying swan – she was poetry in motion and I captured the scene with smoke hazed eyes. She was very much in charge – everything about her was authoritative. She strode in a straight line down the centre of the long, busy corridor, brushing aside barristers and military personnel of all ranks. I couldn't take my eyes off her. One of the American guards told me she was Russian, but wouldn't give any more details. Every time I visited the Palace of Justice after that I looked for her but I never saw her again. She was so different from the otherwise uniformly drab and shabby Russian personnel. Part of the attraction too was that she – unlike most of the females – was unattainable. I spent hours wondering who she was and building up stories about her in my mind.

The sentry duty outside the courthouse was shared between the four allied nations. The Russians wore their forage caps, grey blouse tunics with black belts, ballooned trousers and black jackboots. They looked a mess. I couldn't understand why the Russians allowed such tatty troops to be on general display. Most of them looked Mongolian and I wondered how this untidy rabble could have defeated the German Army. The Russians seemed to cotton on to the situation and the next time their turn came round they put their Red Guard out, dressed in long grey greatcoats, peaked caps with a red star up front, polished boots and white banded, gleaming rifles – very smart indeed.

Generally the German people took very little notice of what was going on in the Palace of Justice; some even seemed to avert their eyes deliberately. The only time I ever saw a crowd gather at the big black iron gates was when a detachment of Scots Guards were being put through their paces by an RSM with a bellow like a bull and vocabulary that made your eyes water. This was luckily being delivered in such a broad Scottish accent that I could only catch the occasional profanity, although the gist was very clear. The pipes were blasting away and the tartan kilts swung as the band marched – the precision of the drill was a delight to watch. Their performance left the rest standing. No one else had a chance when the Brigade of Guards were on duty.

I looked in on the trials again and noticed Goering and Hess having a whispered conversation at one point. I wondered on the turn of events which made us help Stalin and his mob with our convoys and how many men had lost their lives in them. It seemed ironic that Hess was in dock and not Stalin. To me the latter seemed the worse of the two, with his antics at Yalta and his murderous pogroms. I also noticed Herr Schatts, the German financier who had more or less transformed the German economy. How could you try a financial genius for doing his job? Sir Stafford Cripps could have learned a thing or two from that man!

About a week or so after the New Year I was called to the colonel's room and told I had been given compassionate leave as Mum was seriously ill in hospital. 'They've been trying to locate you for a few days, McCarthy, so you'd better get home as soon as you can – there's a plane leaving Furth tomorrow morning and you're on it. You've got a week – good luck.' I stood there, shocked at the news.

I was stunned – as I got myself organised I wondered what was wrong with her. I made a beeline for the American PX shop and bought her the best French perfume I could find and a couple of hundred cigarettes for Dad and myself. Needless to say I didn't sleep too well and was glad to be on my way next morning. Fred and Bill escorted me to the jeep and promised to look after my duties.

It was a small aeroplane and there were only five civilian passengers, a GI and an American army woman officer. I grabbed a seat by a window and we took off as soon as we were all safely seated. I kept thinking about Mum and what was wrong – it was worse not knowing as it gave my imagination plenty to work on. The flight soon became very bumpy and I wondered at times if we were going to make it. I tried to sleep but just as I was nodding off the GI sidled over to me and started chatting.

'Hiya pal, you're a Britisher ain't you?'

'Yeah', I wondered what was coming next.

'You going home?'

'Yes', I replied. 'I'm on compassionate leave, my Mum's very ill.'

'Gee, fella, I'm sorry about your Ma. I'm on compassionate leave too.'

'Are you?', I replied, surprised.

'Yeah, I'm going to get married, but the trouble is I don't know anyone over there. Would you be my best man?'

I was flabbergasted. I hadn't known the guy two minutes and here he was asking me to be his best man!

The American lady officer had overheard this conversation and she was smiling at me.

'But I don't even know your name or your girl. How can I be your best man?'

'Easy, fella. I know you and you're at Nuremburg.'

By now everyone was interested and I looked up to see a half dozen faces turned to me – straining their ears waiting for my reply.

'By the way, fella, what's your name?'

'Mac', I replied, not wanting to give any more information, 'and yours?'

'John.'

'Well look, John, I've got plenty on me plate at the moment.'

'Why I know you have, buddy, but you're the only one I can turn to.'

This guy didn't give up easily. Everyone's eyes turned to me again, waiting my reply.

'Where are you getting married?'

'It's in the North – a place called Knutsford. Have you heard of it?'

'No. I dunno where that is. Even if I said "yes" I've still gotta find the place.'

Johnny sensed I was weakening and everyone leaned a bit closer – I felt cornered.

'Say you'll do it, please buddie.'

I could see he was desperate and I gave in.

'OK Yank, I'll do it.'

Everyone looked relieved and cheered. Why the hell he didn't pick on one of them I don't know!

He started pumping my hand. 'Mac, you're a real pal.'

'Think nothing of it bud – all in a day's work', but the sarcasm was lost on him.

'I'll meet you off the train', he assured me. 'I believe you've got to change at Manchester, but we'll be there to meet you – don't worry.' He pulled out a packet of Camel cigarettes and we celebrated with a smoke.

The turbulence was getting worse and the plane kept dropping – my stomach wasn't enjoying the trip. I looked out of the window and saw that we were crossing some mountains. Later the captain announced that we'd have to land in Belgium for more fuel as the headwind was so strong the plane was using it up fast. It was just one damn thing after another, and I was in a sweat to see Mum. After what seemed ages we caught sight of the white cliffs near Dover – always a grand sight, but especially welcome right then.

We hadn't been told where we were landing and I hoped it wouldn't be too far from London. After a while we began to cross over a built up area and I recognised the city. I could see a red bus looking just like a matchbox toy. On we flew and suddenly I recognised the area below – there was the white roof of the Mayfair cinema on Caledonian Road.

'Blimey, the Mayfair', I shouted, and everyone turned towards me and smiled. Soon we were banking and I realised joyfully, seeing the tube railway lines, that we were going to land at Hendon, the closest aerodrome to home.

As we left the plane the American WAC turned to me quietly. 'Look me up', she said as she handed me a slip of paper with her name on it and the name of the hotel where she was staying.

'Sure honey, if I get time ', I replied. These Yanks didn't waste time! But that was the last I saw of her. When I did find time to see her, I had lost the piece of paper and couldn't remember the name of the hotel. I didn't find her behaviour strange at the time, though. War and its aftermath had a way of dispensing with most of the social 'niceties'.

After the customs officer had looked through our gear I changed the rest of my German currency with one of the officials. He wanted to know how I had got so much money – about 70 quids worth. Luckily he accepted my explanation. Johnny and I left the airport together, both loaded with kitbags.

'Where are you makin' for, Johnny?', I asked him.

'I've got to get to Euston Station', he replied.

'Well get the tube with me from Colindale. I have ter change at Camden Town but the train will take you straight there. How did you meet your girl?' I asked as we walked towards the underground station.

'I was stationed up there', he replied, going on to describe a part of

England I had never been to or even heard of. As the train approached Camden Town we made our final arrangements to meet at the weekend. He put his arm round my shoulder and said quietly, 'Don't forget me, Mac, I'm counting on you.'

As the train pulled into the tunnel with him on it and me on the platform at Camden Town, I wondered what I had let myself in for. I suddenly realised that I was going to have to pay the fare to Knutsford myself. Just as well I had plenty of dough on me. I hadn't been drawing off my paybook for weeks, having made plenty of money in tips and deals.

At last I reached home and knocked on the door of the flat. Dad answered it. 'Wotcher, Dad, it's only me.' It was good to see him.

Dad stared for a moment. 'Blimey, look wot's turned up', he said, with a grin. 'Come on in, Boysie.'

'How's Mum?', I demanded. 'What's it all about? Where is she? In hospital?'

'Yeah, she's in the Archway. Strangulated hernia or something', replied Dad putting the kettle on. 'Did it putting up clean curtains.'

It was a relief to know the facts – I'd been imagining all sorts of things.

''Ave you eaten?', Dad asked.

'No.'

'Wanna sandwich? I've got some cheese.'

'Yes please, and a cuppa tea.'

I rummaged in my kit bag and handed him a pack of 200 cigarettes.

'What cigarettes are these?'

'Them's Lucky Strikes – American cigarettes. There's a bottle of Paris perfume for Mum, hope she likes it.'

'Funny tastin' fags' said Dad as he took a puff.

'Yeah, you'll get used to them – I've got a few more of 'em 'ere somewhere.'

'I must say you look rough, Boysie', he said, peering at me closely. 'You gettin' enough sleep? You wanta take it easy and leave the women alone! Give it a rest son.'

'Sure thing, Dad, sure thing. When can I visit Mum?' I answered, trying to change the subject.

'Tomorrow mornin'. 'Ere's yer tea and sandwich, drink up before it gets cold.'

It was good to sleep in my own bed again. I slept like a log, woke early next morning and spruced myself up. Clutching the precious bottle of perfume, wrapped in a paper bag, off I went. It was nice to wear shoes instead of hobnailed boots. I arrived at the ward and a nurse showed me to Mum's bed. As I tried to walk quietly on the slippery floor all eyes followed me. Never had I felt so conspicuous. After what seemed miles I reached Mum's bed. 'Hullo, Mum', I said, looking anxiously at her. ''Ow long 'ave yer been in 'ere?'

Mum looked up and smiled when she saw me. 'Hullo, Boysie'. Her eyes narrowed as she looked at me. ''Ow did yer get them bags under yer eyes? You bin at it with them German girls?!'

I could feel myself blushing. 'I've brought yer a present', I said and I pushed the paper bag into her hands, hoping she'd change the subject. She opened the bottle and sniffed the perfume. 'That's nice', she smiled. ''Ow much did they rush yer fer that? It's got a lovely smell.

'Put a bit on yer 'ankie', I said. I noticed the bottle was called 'Paris by Night'. We chatted about how she had injured herself. She hadn't gone to the doctor until it was almost too late and had been rushed in for emergency surgery a very sick woman indeed. Luckily she was well on the mend by the time I had arrived. She wanted to know all about the army and looked approvingly at my neat uniform with the bright new insignia which Rosie, the kind-hearted housemaid in the Lawrences' house in Stielen Strasse had sewn on for me only a few nights previously. The words Grenadier Guards almost glowed across my shoulders. Most of the time we wore denim when working and I had a spare utility GG in black I put on the epaulettes.

Mum had obviously been telling her fellow patients about me and leant over to introduce me to her friend in the next bed. As she did so the bottle of perfume rolled off the bed and smashed on the floor. Within seconds the whole ward smelled like a Paris brothel! I dabbed Mum's hankie in it and nurses from all over the place homed in on the pool of rapidly evaporating perfume with hankies, like bees around the honey pot. Any bit of cloth was brought into use and there was a pushing and shoving mass of women in the gap between the beds before you could say 'Jack Robinson'. Talk about chaos! Worse still, some had splashed on my trouser leg and I got more than one funny look over the next few days.

Mum told me later that for weeks after the nurses and patients were still smelling of 'Paris by Night' and talking about the incident. It was the sweetest smelling ward in London for days.

I took dad to Wimbledon dog track that evening and gave him some money to bet with. It was great to see him dodging in and out around the bookmakers' stands trying to get the best odds on the dog he fancied. I fancied one in the fourth race, I remember it was in trap 6 – the dog with the striped jacket.

'Dad, try to get 6-1 for me while I get the drinks in.' I handed him one of those crinkly crisp white fivers – one of those they said was as good as a passport in the old days. Dad scrutinised the fiver as if it was the Death Warrant of Charles the First.

'Boysie, this is more than a week's wages!'

'I know, Dad – try and get the best odds.'

He disappeared and after a while returned with a grin. 'We got it.'

'Sixes.'

'Yus.'

The lights were dimmed and the hare started its lurching journey round the track. The crowd roared and believe it or not my dog scraped home! Before I could react, Dad had disappeared – to return a minute or so later with a fistful of notes.

'The bookie says try someone else next time', he chortled. I bunged a tenner into Dad's top pocket and we went to the bar for a celebratory drink before going home winners for a change.

The next day I had to get to Knutsford – how I wished I hadn't allowed myself to be persuaded, it was so good being home. I rang Johnny and told him which train I'd be on. I got out at Manchester and stood on the platform – no Johnny. 'Sod it', I fumed and thought I'd better find out how I could get to Knutsford. Then the cloud of steam dispersed sufficiently for me to see GI Johnny running towards me, waving 'Over here, Mac, over here.' He hugged me. 'Boy, am I glad to see you. I thought you mighta chickened out, you son of a gun.'

'Nope, I even paid my fare', I replied, hoping the penny would drop. No chance, but I reckoned he needed all his dough for the wedding, so I didn't labour the point.

'Come and meet my girl's sisters, let's take your bag.'

'No, that's OK, it isn't heavy.' I was a bit embarrassed at all this attention and hugging.

He introduce me to Hilda and Gladys and we had a drink before going for the Knutsford train. I'd never been that way before and looked out of the window, conscious all the while of the stares of the two girls. 'Why did I ever volunteer?', I thought to myself, feeling uncomfortable under their gaze.

Eventually we reached Knutsford. As we walked from the station together, Johnny seemed subdued – probably wedding nerves. It had been arranged that I stay overnight at the mother-in-law's house and I hadn't been there long before I was introduced to the bride-to-be. It didn't need good eyesight to see that she was extremely pregnant! I found Johnny and caught him by the arm. 'She's in the puddin' club!', I hissed. 'Why didn't you tell me she was in the family way!?'

'I'm sorry, Mac', said Johnny, looking sheepish. 'I thought that you'd let me down. Honest to God, pal, that's why I got compassionate leave.'

'Yeah, too much bloody passion', I retorted. 'Come on, it's time we were leaving for the registry office.'

'Got the ring, Mac?'

'Sure! I ought to put it through your nose!'

It was a pretty dull affair, the outfits restricted to what was available and how many coupons had been saved. Most of the younger men were in khaki. The reception was held in what seemed to be a double-fronted shop. The women had got together and done their best to do the happy couple proud, but it was like trying to make a swan out of a small duckling. It was a good humoured affair but I felt a stranger – I didn't even know Johnny's surname! The toasts were drunk and I was just beginning to relax when some drunken slob said 'How about a speech from the best man!'

I was dreading that moment and cringed.

'Yeah, come on. Speech', yelled some woman.

I pushed my chair back and reluctantly stood up. 'Ahem. Ladies and gentlemen', I muttered.

'Speak up! Can't hear you', someone shouted.

'I would like to propose a toast to Johnny and . . . ' I had forgotten the bride's name.

Johnny whispered, 'Margaret.'

Thank God!

'I would like to toast Johnny and Margaret and wish the happy couple all the best for the future.' And I sat down sweating. That's all they were going to get out of me!

'Hear, hear', someone hollered.

'That wasn't a very good speech', the mother-in-law commented audibly.

'Well, I could have said may all your troubles be little ones – but I didn't, did I?'

I'd only known them a couple of hours! It would have been easier to recite Henry V's Agincourt speech than to make one about these two. I didn't know a bloody thing about them! I gradually cooled down as the alcohol relaxed me and the rest of the evening passed pleasantly enough. I had a room and a bed to myself and slept soundly until I was awakened by mother-in-law with a cup of tea the next morning. After breakfast I made my way thankfully back to the Smoke.

On the Monday I had to report first thing to 20 Eaton Square to find out where I was to go for my flight back. As I signed in my papers were closely scrutinised by a couple of police officers at the desk in the hall. A moment later an official looking bloke in a pin-striped suit came down the stairs. 'This way please', he said, and I followed him up the stairs into an office. He seemed to know all about me and gave me

written instructions to report to Odiham Aerodrome near Hook in
Hampshire.

I left Eaton Square and made for Waterloo Station where I got a train
to Hook. I walked for some time along the country roads after asking
an old man for directions, and it was some time before I finally came
upon the airfield. I had to show my paybook and instructions to the
sentry before he would let me pass, and I was escorted to a wooden
hut where there were several other people already gathered. I discovered before long that this was a Canadian Air Force base. Soon afterwards we heard the sound of an aircraft and looking out saw a Dakota
taxiing towards us. Most of the passengers were civilians; some looked
like pressmen, some had transatlantic accents and others, those with
official looking briefcases, must have been civil servants.

It didn't take long to board the plane and get settled in. The seating
accommodation was basic to say the least – simple wooden benches
along either side of the fuselage. The plane was returning to the aerodrome at Furth, so I would be fairly close to home once we had landed
– about four miles from Nuremburg. The Dakota revved up and taxied
for what seemed ages before it eventually took off and banked. Some
trees came into view and I'm positive the undercarriage hit them –
they were so close I could have touched them. The plane seemed to
lurch and most of us looked white and sick. We all sensed that we had
had a narrow escape. For a long time we flew very low across fields,
and the way my guts were reacting to the fright I could have done
some farmer a favour by dropping shit on his fields.

Eventually the plane climbed and the tension in the passenger sec-
tion relaxed. Dad had made me a couple of dripping doorsteps to take
with me and my stomach settled enough for me to tuck in and enjoy
them.

We crossed the French coast and after a long time picked up a large
river and followed that for many miles, heading south – it must have
been the Rhine. Towards the end of the journey the turbulence built
up suddenly and we sat there not knowing whether to cry or be sick as
the plane dropped and heaved. The terrific noise didn't help. Conversation was impossible and it was getting very cold as well as rough, so
I decided to try to sleep. I tipped my peaked cap over my nose so that
all I could see as I dozed off was a pair of very tasty legs in black silk
stockings belonging to the young woman across the fuselage.

A change in the noise of the engines woke me and we discovered
that we were approaching Furth. The Canadian navigator jokingly told
us to hang onto the sides as the old warhorse banked and dipped and
made a perfect landing. I jumped off the plane with relief and got
through customs no bother – all I had brought back with me were a

natty pair of shoes – brown with a narrow black line down the middle which I had brought straight from the the Oxford Shoe Company – and a supply of Durex. I also had a few bits and pieces that would sell on the black market, like soap, coffee, shaving gear and Virginia tobacco and cigarettes. I wanted to get straight to Zirndorf, so I got a lift to the junction where the roads parted and from there I thumbed a lift home.

Fred was the first one I clapped eyes on when I arrived.

'Hello Fred, how's yer love life mate?', I greeted him.

'Need you ask?', he replied.

'You're not goin' to marry her still, are yer?'

'Course I am, when I get the time ter fill in all those bloody forms – whole bleedin' pile of them. By the way – the old man wants ter see you.'

'Right you are Fred.' I smarmed my hair down, made sure I was tidy and tapped on the old man's door.

'Come in.' I walked in.

'Hullo McCarthy. How's your mother? Your father been knocking her about had he?'

I was speechless and stared hard at him trying to control my temper.

'Is that all, sir', I said through gritted teeth.

'No.' He hesitated, sensing that he had upset me. 'Is your mother well?'

'Yes sir. Much better.'

'By the way, I am going on a short trip for some field sport and I want two volunteers to accompany me. I want you and Guardsman Jones to make up the party.'

'What will our duties be, Sir?'

'Beaters.'

'I don't know what you mean, sir.' The crafty sod wanted a favour – after what he'd just said!

'And by the way, I want you to resume taking care of me', he said, ignoring my last comment. Fred must have been giving him nightmares with all the paperwork over his German girl friend.

'Right, sir.' I held out my hand.

'What do you want now', he demanded.

'You owe me 5 marks from last time, Sir.'

'Oh – do I?'

'Yes, sir.'

'You've got a good memory.'

'Sir', I said. I needed one, I thought, with that mean old bugger. He counted me out 5 marks, handed them over and dismissed me curtly.

A couple of weeks later a jeep pulled up outside the house early in the morning with Jones in the front seat acting as the driver. He was in charge of Lt. Col. Mervyn Griffith-Jones, one of our prosecuting team. I sat in front with him, the colonel and a Major Barrington behind. The colonel got a map out and started giving instructions to Jones – we had no idea where we were going because we weren't told.

I was still feeling belligerent towards the colonel, but I gave up and settled back to enjoy the scenery. We were heading east, along roads that a few years before had carried thousands of tanks and troops on their way to their dream of a Third Reich, smashing and destroying anything that opposed them. Now we were busy trying the leaders of that dream, twenty-one or so pathetic men huddled together in a courtroom, knowing damn well what their fate was to be.

As the jeep trundled along through thick forests of pine trees I heard the colonel mention Bohemia and asked him if that was in Czechoslovakia.

'Well according to this map it is', he replied.

Later they swapped seats with us and the major took the wheel – much to our relief – as we relaxed in the back, smoking and enjoying the view. We stopped and stretched our legs and had a 'jimmy riddle'. It was so quiet in the country that you could hear a pin drop.

'Not so far away now, men' said the old man after a while.

'Thank Gawd for that', I muttered to Jones.

After a quarter of an hour or so of hard driving we turned into a large gateway and drove up a long driveway bordered on either side with thick forest. At last we pulled up outside a mansion, a bit like a Scottish castle, complete with pepperpot turrets – very large and very gaunt. We had just reached the front door when it was flung open and down the front steps came an apparition in lederhosen, embroidered blouse, multicoloured waistcoat and a small green trilby topped with a huge feather – just like something out of an American movie. This was the baron, the owner of this ancient pile. He doffed his hat and shook the colonel and major by the hand while we stood there wide eyed, fascinated by the dumpy little figure. Now that his hat was off we could see his shock of black frizzy hair. The baron and the officers moved into the castle and a manservant showed us into the kitchen and introduced us to the cook – a huge woman you needed a map to get past. We exchanged pleasantries in German and communicated quite well once we got her to speak slowly. We sat down at the far end of the huge kitchen table and relaxed.

'This place looks like Dracula's headquarters', commented Jones, looking round, and I must admit he had a point. I could just imagine Bela Lugosi climbing in through the window by the sink.

We had just finished our hot drinks when the manservant Ernst reappeared and told us that they were leaving for the shoot and that we should meet them on the front drive. The baron and the officers had shotguns under their arms and we all squeezed into the jeep. The baron gave instructions and we set off. Soon we were in the heart of the forest. We got out and followed the baron's rotund figure into the thick woods. I was surprised how much light there was under the trees. The three of us lackeys, me, Jonesy and Ernst, were armed with long stakes, but I wished I had my rifle with me. We moved ahead about 20 yards apart, shaking everything in sight, pinecones and dead wood snapping as they were crushed under our boots. Apart from our movements and voices the only other noise was birdsong and the fluttering sound of birds' wings flapping as they flew away from us. Goodness knows what a Scots ghillie would have made of our attempts at beating – I don't think he would have been impressed.

We heard a rustle ahead of us and suddenly there was a shout followed by a snort and the sound of a large animal moving fast through the tangle of lower branches and undergrowth. Three of them fired but they must have missed as there was no sound other than that of the retreating animal.

'Did you see anything, Ernst?'

The manservant shook his head and gesticulated with his hands. 'Grosser swine', he said, pointing. 'He means "big pig"', I thought.

'Did you see anything, Jonesy?', I asked as he came over.

'Honest to God, Mac, that was a bear.'

'A bear – my arse! You're havin us on.'

'No – straight up, I'm sure it was.' He wasn't joking.

'That's dodgy', I said. 'All we've got are these sticks.'

By now the three of them had reloaded and we were sent ahead again – very gingerly this time. It wasn't very funny any more. Deeper and deeper into the forest we went and I began to hope that the baron knew his way back.

Soon there was another rustle and a crash in the undergrowth and the three of them went forward again. I could hear the baron's voice getting very excited. Whatever it was out there I made sure I was well behind their shotguns. Our job was over for a short while and the three of us relaxed. I bunged Ernst a fag as we lit up. I gazed round as I puffed – rays of light added to the beauty of the scene.

The peace was broken by the colonel and the major returning, barking 'Put those cigarettes out! We don't want the wood going up in smoke.' We said nothing as we carefully stubbed out our cigarettes, but mentally our reaction was 'Bollocks!'

Again we sallied forth, almost immediately disturbing something else. This time they fired and there was a squeal and then silence.

'They've hit something', Jonesy said and we moved forward.

'What is it?', I asked as we stood round the dead creature. I'd never seen anything like it.

'A wild boar', answered the baron, who spoke good English.

'Wot – a pig, you mean?'

'Sort of', replied Jones. 'Looks a bit like one round the face.'

The baron pulled a rope from his large pouch and searched with Ernst for a stout branch. He soon found one and quickly had the boar lashed firmly onto the branch.

'OK, men, get that to the jeep and report back as quick as you can.'

'Carry that!' I was flabbergasted, as they moved off again; the beast must have weighed at least three hundredweight by my reckoning. 'What d'you reckon Jonesy?'

Jonesy was scratching his head. 'Search me – it sure is fat.'

'Fat – course its blinking fat. It's a fat pig!'

We heaved the branch onto our shoulders and staggered back towards the jeep, the boar swinging between us and throwing us off balance. The weight was incredible and why the branch didn't snap was anyone's guess. The path back was rough, over small streams and through thick undergrowth. We cursed and sweated and the branch bruised our shoulders. We got back to the jeep eventually.

'Want a Phillip Morris?', queried Jonesy as we got our breath back.

'Nah – can't stand the taste.'

'Suit yerself', he replied, lighting up and flopping down under a big tree to enjoy it.

'This takes the bloody biscuit ', I stormed as I flopped down beside him. 'All they bloody well wanted was a couple of meat porters – know what I mean? Just like bleedin' Smithfield Market.'

We sat there while Jonesy finished his fag and reluctantly decided to get back, knowing the officers would be timing us. The poor old boar lay next to the jeep seeping blood from the bullet holes. As slowly as we dared we walked back towards the noises of voices and shots, hoping to goodness they didn't manage to shoot anything else! I had left my cap in the jeep and the low branches scratched my face and scalp as we beat our way further into the forest. I couldn't win.

We were getting very tired and hungry by now and I had just turned to wave to Ernst on the right flank when suddenly an enormous wild boar charged at us out of a thick patch of undergrowth. For a second we froze then we dived for cover behind the nearest tree, leaving the guns behind free to fire. It snorted and swerved, trying to attack on several fronts at once. Its swerving saved its life. They missed and the boar, deciding that discretion was the better part of valour, turned and ran off into the gloom and safety. To our enormous relief they decided to call it a day and we trudged wearily back to the jeep talking about the one that got away.

The dead boar was quite a problem. There were six of us crunched up in the jeep already and we couldn't work out how to get it back to the castle. We tried to lash it over the bonnet but that didn't work. In the end we lashed it over the back of the spare wheel with the colonel, the major and the baron holding onto the rope and Ernst up front balancing the weight!

Dinner wouldn't be ready for at least an hour after we arrived back so the cook gave us a very welcome glass of schnapps. We were to eat in the kitchen – much to our relief. We were starving by then. After a while I fancied a stroll to take a look round. Jonesy declined the offer to join me, having taken his boots off. I set off round the grounds on my own – it was beautiful countryside and I enjoyed my stroll. A path through woodland took me to the crest of a ridge which overlooked a valley with a hamlet in the bottom. I looked slowly round, enjoying the peace and quiet, but as I moved along the ridge the view was extended and suddenly spoiled. In a clearing in the woods on the opposite slopes was one of the familiar camps surrounded by barbed wire. I couldn't believe it. Suddenly the place, as beautiful as it was, became devoid of charm. I felt a chill in the air. The place looked deserted from where I stood and I told myself it was an old POW camp, but my instinct wasn't fooled. I turned to go back, my walk thoroughly spoiled.

The cook did us proud with great steaming plates of food; there was no evidence of the shortage that was such a feature around Nuremburg. The vegetables were fresh – maybe they grew their own. We noshed away, elbows well to the fore, making short work of the food that Ernst served us. We mopped the delicious gravy with hunks of homemade black bread, the likes of which I hadn't tasted before. The plates were cleared away by a scullery maid and we sat back, undid our belts and relaxed.

Everything in that huge kitchen was larger than life size. The table was getting on for a full size snooker table, the dresser held dozens of full size plates and countless other pieces of china. Even the cook was extra large!

I mentioned the camp I had seen to the cook, who stopped and looked at me with a tense expression on her face. 'Nix gut! Nix gut!' she said, shaking her head. I asked her if it was a prison for soldiers.

'Nein', she replied. She looked round, finding that no one was there but us. 'Juden. Juden.'

'Jews! ... My Gawd', I gasped, my worst fears realised. 'Even here!' She pointed to a lamp on a side table which had a shade that resembled vellum. 'Juden', she said again, pointing to the shade and stroking her skin. Was there only one conclusion? My flesh began to creep.

'I don't believe this', Jonesy said grimly.

The cook then picked up the bar of soap we had washed our hands and faces with when we had come in. 'Seif [soap]. Juden, seif.' We knew what she meant and looked at each other aghast, not wanting to believe what we were hearing. We wanted to think she was mistaken, but this big old woman was deadly serious, there was no mistaking the expression in her big brown eyes. We thanked her for the superb dinner and got outside as quickly as we could for some fresh air. We were both feeling sick. That beautiful peaceful valley had held that awful place. They must have known what was going on.

The colonel and the major arrived and we set off back to Zirndorf. It was a sombre journey and the grim realities of war and the significance of what the trials were all about took on a new reality and a new meaning for me.

One afternoon Harry and I decided to explore the old city of Nuremburg, as we both had time off together. I showed him round the Palace of Justice first – he was able to get in because he had a pass too, issued when we'd all been summoned there to get the paperwork done. I kept my eyes skinned for that gorgeous and flamboyant Russian woman, but there was no sign of her. I took him into a recently opened library which was run by Christine Rommel, niece of Rommel of the Afrika Korp – the Desert General. I had tried to date her but didn't quite make it – too many flashy GI romeos with the same idea. We visited the public gallery to watch the trials. Harry put on the headphones and I kept moving the switch from one language to another, enjoying the expression on his face and the grin when I turned it to English and he suddenly understood what was going on.

When we had completed our tour we strolled into the old city which, despite the bomb damage, was still impressive. Antiquated wooden buildings, huge churches and cobbled squares surrounded us. I could just imagine Martin Luther coming round the corner to hammer his complaints on the door of the Catholic church.

Having had our fill of culture we decided to top up with booze in a bar which had recently opened and was very popular just then. There were plenty of girls there and we spent the evening getting more and more sloshed. Eventually we staggered out into the night. Curfew was long past so I suggested we stayed at the Grand Hotel for the night with Jacko, but Harry was on early duty at Zirndorf and needed to get back. We both decided to walk. We hadn't staggered more than 200 yards when an American jeep pulled up alongside and the two of us were unceremoniously pushed protesting into the back seat by a couple of burly military policemen. After a short drive we pulled into a courtyard and were bundled into a cell which already held about half a dozen inmates. The heavy door was slammed behind us and the bolts shot home. Harry and I stared at each other in dismay.

I was the first to find my voice. 'It's a bleedin' nick, 'Arry. A soddin' prison. Those f...in' Yanks 'ave locked us up!' We looked round us and noted the unsavoury characters in the dim light. They were equally interested in the new arrivals. We retreated into the one remaining empty corner. 'We'd better not kip 'Arry', I poked him as he was nodding off. I'd heard too many stories about life in these cells. It then hit me that we could be here for weeks. 'Sod this for a lark', I thought, 'if we don't make a stand now we could be here indefinitely.' 'Come on 'Arry, let's wake the sods up!' I went to the door and banged and hollered until one of the 'screws' came to see what the commotion was about. 'Hey, buddy, when are we gettin' outa here?' I demanded.

'Look pal, hold onto yer shirt, take it easy fella, just calm down or you'll wake the dead up! We usually let you out of the lock up if you're clean. You were caught out after curfew.'

'Big deal, soldier! Sorry, pal, no offence meant – we just wanna know when we can get out of this damn calaboose.'

I was relieved to hear we'd be out in the morning and turned to give Harry the good news. He had fallen asleep again and was snoring his head off with his back against the cell bars.

Sure enough, the next morning we were on the line up, our ID cards checked and Harry and I, together with a motley collection of prostitutes, squaddies with hangovers and other repulsive looking characters, were turned out of the massive prison door onto the early morning street. I think we had been held in a part of the same prison that was holding the Nazi prisoners on trial. We managed to hitch a lift into Zirndorf, so no one was any the wiser. We both felt lousy and tired after our night in that crummy jail and the minute we could we took hot baths and hit the sack. Fred, sharing the attic with me, obviously knew I had not been in overnight – he was probably getting used to it – and wanted to know what had happened. He'd heard that we'd been picked up – the Bahnhof Express had rumbled by just as we were being hustled into the jeep and the driver had recognised us.

'Just think', he grinned, 'you could've 'ad a ride in the back wiv' all that crumpet.'

I groaned at the thought "Onest, Fred, I don't think we could've managed 'em the state we were in; beside, why spoil the old 'uns their pleasure.' I told him to wake me in a couple of hours with a cuppa.

The black market continued to thrive and I was doing well selling shaving soap, soap, chocolate, cigarettes, Solingen steel cut-throat razors – you name it, I sold it. This part of Germany had a reputation for mechanical toys and cameras, Leicas in particular, both rare and very valuable commodities just then. I did most of my trading in Nuremburg as I got much higher prices there for my goods, but I still did a little business with Hans, the stoker. We sometimes sat by the fire and he'd tell me about his time on the Eastern front. He would rub his hands together and shiver violently and say 'Kalt' and tell me how the diesel oil froze in the tanks, immobilising them. Then he'd get up and put another shovel of coal onto the fire of the boiler, as if to make up for those awful times.

I had almost forgotten about the football match we'd arranged when a message was sent telling me that it was definitely on and asking if I would play. The match was to be against the French Army and it was a needle match, so I put in as much training as I could and had some early nights in the week or so I had left. The Soldiers Field had been booked for the occasion – the famous stadium in Nuremburg where Hitler addressed his Nazi followers in their thousands and where their banner-bedecked marches and rallies had been such a feature during the 1930s.

On the day of the match we left for the field with a crowd of supporters. We managed to get a complete kit together of white shirts and our navy PT shorts, but try as we might, we couldn't get any football boots. I took my army boots and my plimsolls and as the pitch turned out to be dry, wore the latter. I made a couple of shin pads out of cardboard. Two waggon loads of us set off in high spirits and hell bent on victory.

'You've gotta beat those Froggies' was the instruction from the team manager when we were finally all assembled. 'You OK Mac?' he asked, looking closely at my face.

'Yeah, fine.'

'You look a bit pasty. You sure you're OK? We need you to make the team up', he said jokingly.

'Gee, thanks! I need all the encouragement I can get. You big stiff!'

After another close look he relaxed and told me my job was to beat the full back down the line and get my crosses in.

We had a good team with four professionals in. One played for Glasgow Rangers and another for Celtic – I can't remember who the other two played for – but it was reassuring to know they were there.

When we arrived the French team were already there. The arena was enormous – certainly the biggest I had played on. On the far side the Yanks had drawn out a baseball pitch.

The game kicked off and I very quickly discovered I had a big guy playing at right back facing me all the time. Every time I tried to dart past him he crunched me – several times in the first twenty minutes I had to pick myself up off the floor after being dumped there by him. I decided to change my tactics and slowed down with the ball so that I could take evasive action. The ploy worked and he got fed up as I swerved my shoulders and with the double shuffle got him going the wrong way so I could get past him. The first time this succeeded he said something in French as I swept past. I don't think it was 'Bonjour'.

Soon I was able to sling a long ball in to Lecombie, the ex-Celtic player who thumped it in from twenty yards for our first goal, just before half time. It was a tough match by any standards – they too had a good team and the second half was very tightly contested. I had been given orders to continue sending over as many centres from the left wing as possible and this was what I continued to do. Despite the very cold weather we were sweating and steaming – shirts wet and clinging clammily to our bodies. Soon after resuming play the French levelled the score. Both sets of supporters yelled their team on and the Yanks, who had come to see what this weird game was like, took sides and yelled too. In one movement I got a hefty kick on the ankle – a part not covered by the cardboard – which had me hobbling for a while, but the excitement of the game deadened the pain and I was soon back in action, sticking my arse out at any Frog who came near while I was shielding the ball. Towards the end we won a corner and I took it and tried to swerve it into the goal. Someone got his head to it and in it went, into the net for the winning goal. We were chuffed, backslapping and laughing, when the final whistle blew. The strength of our team had certainly been the presence of the four pros and the confidence they had given the rest of us. We weren't able to train together at all, yet we had gelled as a team. We savoured that match and victory for a long time.

8

The Nuremburg War Trials

A few days after the match I was transferred again – this time to work with my old mate Jacko in the Grand Hotel. The trials were now in full swing and visiting VIPs from all over were staying at the hotel. Jacko and I were there to see to their needs while they were in Nuremburg.

I said goodbye to Fred and his girlfriend at Zirndorf, slung a kitbag into the first truck I could find going to Nuremburg and set off – glad to be going to a place where there was more action.

Jacko had been a mate of mine for a long time and I was delighted to be working with him. He was a real character and up to more fiddles than the London Symphony Orchestra. His uniform was exclusively GI issue and he had contacts throughout the city. He took me round and introduced me to the staff of the hotel. There was the chief receptionist whom we called Fritz, an old boy with slick grey hair and steel-rimmed spectacles, natty in a morning suit, plus a couple of lift boys, and the porters. As I was introduced to each one there was all this handshaking – a custom I found tedious to say the least, as it happened so often. Then we continued the tour of the hotel, me making a mental note of the location of the bathroom, stairs and service rooms, etc.

Our room, 301, faced the side street and overlooked the bombed cinema. It was pretty basic – two single beds with small cabinets, wash basin, cupboard, occasional table and telephone – but compared with many in the town it was luxury. I was introduced to the old lady who cleaned the bedroom, her cleaning room being opposite ours. 'Keep in with her', warned Jacko. 'She makes us a cuppa when she's on duty.'

On the far side of the hotel I was shown the laundry and dry cleaning service room – the mainstay of the hotel – run by a couple of Southern GIs, Cox and Renfrew. Jacko told me that Renfrew – a tall very bronzed bloke with black hair – was a full-blooded Red Indian.

'On yeah', I retorted, not believing him. 'And what do you call him, Geronimo?'

'No, straight up, Mac, 'e's supposed to be a kind of chieftain. '

'Sure thing, Jacko.'

It was fascinating to meet my first Red Indian – they were both great guys and we had a good chat before we left. 'Take it easy, fellas', one of them called out as we left.

'You bet', I said, nodding my head.

'I'll show you the mess room on the way up', said Jacko as we climbed the back stairs. 'Take a 'bo-peep' at this he said, and opened a door off the dusty staircase.

We went through the door onto a small balcony which overlooked a polished wooden dance floor. Spotlights fixed onto the edge of the balcony lit up the floor when shone onto a large multifaceted mirror globe that turned and sent splinters of light swirling round the room. It was called the Marble Room – although I don't remember seeing any marble there.

'Cor – I'd like to see this place in full swing', I said, as we stood and listened to a band practising.

'It's strictly for officers', replied Jacko.

'Of course', I replied sarcastically.

In the basement was the restaurant for us servicemen and the food stores which I already knew well, as we got our supplies for the judges' houses here.

I was also introduced to a couple of waiters.

'That one buys cigarettes', said Jacko, nodding in the direction of a smaller youth. 'How much do you get for yours?'

'About 400 marks', I replied.

'Chicken feed', he retorted. 'I get 800.'

'I don't believe it!'

'Straight up. Would I kid you?'

'That's about four marks a fag.' Holy mackerel!

'Watch him', Jacko warned. 'He's a son of a bitch.'

He'd got all the American patter, had Jacko, and he could charm his way through any situation. He'd fought all through the Italian campaign and come out without a scratch.

While retracing our steps we passed the GI guard on the back door and I was duly introduced. As we went up the stairs the guard hollered something to Jacko that I didn't catch. Jacko started to laugh and explained. 'He caught me fetching up a bint the other night – strictly verboten – some will look the other way if they know you – others won't – he's OK.'

Back in room 301 he poured us a whisky apiece – he had everything he needed there!

'Who's staying here at the moment that I should know about?' I asked. Jacko paused and thought. 'A couple of generals, several newspaper wallahs – Oh, and Dame Laura Knight. She's got a couple of rooms through the back past the scaffolding – nice old girl.' He filled me in on the job. We had to check all arrivals and departures, not just by asking the reception staff but checking the register and bookings to make doubly sure. Check the maids had done their jobs in the rooms and keep the door locked, especially at night – too many at the thieving stakes. 'Oh, there's an American film star staying too – what's his name – Tyrone Power – got a gorgeous bird with him. Let's get some chow and then I'll take yer down to Captain Casson – he usually lets us know whose coming to stay.'

'But what do I do for them?' I queried.

'Oh – clean their shoes, see that they've got everything they want, tell them where things are – you know – just fix things for 'em, make them feel comfortable.'

'Doesn't sound much.'

'You just wait – you'd be surprised! There's so many comin' and goin' it gets very hectic. You've got to eat when you can and manage as best as you can when they're all turnin' up at once', Jacko warned. 'We'd better get down and see Captain Casson now before we eat, before it gets too late.' Straightening ourselves up, Jacko led the way downstairs.

'Mind you – Casson's a bit odd.'

'Odd?' I queried.

'Yeah – doesn't go for the women, if you know what I mean.'

'You're joking!'

'I'm not, just see fer yourself – that's all.' He knocked on the door and a voice called out to come in.

'Who's there?', the voice enquired as we walked into the room.

'It's me – Jacko – Sir. I've got McCarthy with me.'

I was busy looking round – I couldn't see anyone in the room. Then I caught sight of Captain Casson – sitting on the bog in full view of the room with his trousers round his ankles, the door to the bathroom wide open.

'Sit down both of you, I won't keep you a minute.'

We sat down and Jacko grinned and winked at me. Soon Captain Casson came in, busy doing up his flies.

'Yes Jacko – what can I do for you?'

Jacko introduced me and told him I'd be a part of the team. I knew Casson already from Zirndorf and he recognised me. He was a bit on the porky side with thinning hair and metal rimmed glasses, and he had a transatlantic accent – not quite American, more Canadian. He checked with us who was in and gave a few instructions as we enjoyed the whisky he poured us.

We left soon after and as we walked along the corridor Jacko said, 'Do you know, he gets very lonely at times. It must be difficult not liking the ladies.'

'Why not fix him up with Jughead for a wrestle in the gym – he'd find it a gripping experience. Ol' Jughead won't mind, it'll keep him in practice.' Our mate Jughead was one of the best Cornish wrestlers around.

After a quick meal of sausage and chips, we went out of the back door to a nearby bar for a drink. 'Always use the back or side entrance of the hotel, out of sight – out of mind', instructed Jacko, as we clattered down the back stairs and out onto the cobbled street. We walked across the main road and into the beer cellar.

'Do you know, Jacko, the last time I sat and had a drink here with the lads, I remember the kraut band struck up the Star Spangled Banner and everyone stood, except us.' We couldn't make out why – then it suddenly dawned on us it was the Yanks' national anthem – we stood to attention with the rest. I don't think any of us had heard it before.

We spent a pleasant evening listening to the band and chatting up the frauleins and then we walked back to the hotel. As we passed the central station I looked over and stopped in my tracks.

'Bloody hell, it's the Bahnhof Express! They must be working overtime!' It was nice to know it was still going.

Over the next few days I tried to get to know the place – the back was still being rebuilt and was a mess, but the public areas in the main part were as plush and luxurious as could be. I would station myself by the pot plants near the foot of the staircase and watch the activity. There were all kinds of people coming and going – people from all corners of the earth, famous and unknown, servicemen and women and civilians. A few Russians came in, but they kept very much to themselves – they lived on the outskirts of town where they held numerous parties and drank lots of vodka. We were never invited.

Back at the hotel a few days later, 'Fritz', the chief receptionist (I never knew his real name), told me to expect a general the next day. I checked the hotel register and found that it was General Laycock, who was the chief of Combined Operations. I was going up in the world – minder to a general!

A week or so after joining him at the Grand Hotel, Jacko went on leave and I was left in charge. Typically he had managed to fiddle a flight home (he knew the right sort of Americans) instead of the tedious and unreliable train and boat. I got our room shipshape then checked on who was leaving or arriving. I polished several pairs of shoes, some Sam Brownes and tidied rooms a bit. Some of the visitors were actually leaving their shoes outside their rooms at night to be polished – a rash thing to do as shoes couldn't be bought for love or money and the temptation to nick them must have been overwhelming. It was mostly the Americans who put their shoes out and it struck me that they were very naive – devastation and crippling poverty, shortages everywhere, and they left shoes on public corridors expecting them to be there the next morning polished! I could only assume that they had just flown in from the States and hadn't yet caught up with the reality of war-ravaged Europe.

A couple of days after I assumed charge the telephone rang and 'Fritz' informed me in his clipped accent that another general would be arriving the next day. On checking the register, I discovered that the name looked like General Brian Horrocks, so I had two generals as guests. All I needed was a field marshal to make it a hat trick!

I nipped up to the new arrival's room to see if everything was OK and popped along the corridor to see General Laycock, who asked me if I could get his uniform cleaned. I noticed a book on his bedside table – it was called the *Horned Pigeon*. I promised myself I would read it one day. He was a very pleasant gentleman to have dealings with – he found time to talk and to listen.

While only officers could go to the cabaret, other ranks and hotel staff could stand on the balcony and enjoy the scene. I often spent time during the evenings there – laughing at the comedians or simply enjoying the beauties in their evening dresses on the tiny dance floor as the music played softly below. There was a great atmosphere on the balcony, jam packed in the dark; the cigarette smoke hung like a cloud through the spotlight beams as we took it all in. The voices of the German maids singing to the music of the band made it magical. Every day I kept Captain Casson informed as to who had arrived – there were so many to deal with that I asked for another helper and he promised to arrange it.

During a lull in the flurry of activity I decided to visit the trials again and was walking there when I heard someone calling my name. I looked round and saw Johnny – the GI whose best man I had been in Knutsford. I crossed the road and was greeted effusively by him. 'Hiya pal! Remember me? What gives? Say it's good to see you, Mac, I didn't think I'd ever see you again.'

I couldn't believe it. Of all the squaddies on Nuremburg High Street, and there were plenty, GI Johnny stood out radiantly.

'Hi there, Johnny, you ol' son of a gun', I replied. 'How's the wife?'

'She's fine – she's going Stateside as soon as the kid's born.'

'Well, it's nice to meet an ol' married man', I quipped. 'How long have you bin back?'

'Oh, a few weeks now, and I'll be glad to catch that boat back home pronto out of this dump', he said looking around.

'I'm goin' ter watch the trials – you comin'?'

'No way! I don't wanna watch that bullshit.' He hugged me and thanked me again for coming up trumps in his hour of need. 'Take care of yourself now, y'hear, s'long' and off he went. I never saw him again.

As I approached the Palace of Justice the usual array of tanks and jeeps were dotted around its perimeter. I wondered why – the Germans seemed to take not a blind bit of notice of what was going on. They were too busy surviving – as they plodded by, eyes often downcast, they reminded me of fans of a beaten cup final side leaving Wembley. Mind you, there were a good many Germans employed by the Americans inside the place – 'trustees' they were called.

That afternoon the yellow-skinned prisoners seemed more confident – almost like actors playing parts for the gaggle of news-cameras. The star was, as usual, Goering, brash and self-confident as he studied sheets of paper. Strutting to the dock in his grey uniform, baggy trousers and polished jackboots, for one brief moment, I got the impression that if he had had a cane he would have smacked his boots with it! Hair plastered down with almost a centre parting, he held the stage – he was going down with all guns blazing. He was to be cross examined by Mr Justice Robert Jackson, the chief American prosecutor, and as it was the Yank's show the place was packed. But from the dock Goering tore him to shreds on every conceivable point – much to the chagrin of the rest of us, especially the Yanks. Goering was making a meal of it with wads of paper and long speeches. This was going to take a long time, we all sensed. Justice Jackson just didn't succeed in his cross examination. We all squirmed in our seats. Goering was a wily old campaigner, and had the American prosecutor on the ropes. Jackson never recovered from this humiliation. Goering also made mincemeat of the French and the Russian prosecutors, and you could sense the alarm at this turn of events. I could see the trials going on forever. Looking round the packed balcony I could see despondency amongst those sitting there. The British were next on the list and I and many others were hoping they would redress the balance for the English-speaking world, after the fiasco with Justice Robert Jackson.

The prisoners were being tried on four counts, conspiracy for war, crimes against peace, war crimes and crimes against humanity, and they were using every opportunity to debate issues and deliver long speeches. It was only when Sir David Maxwell-Fyffe and Sir Hartley Shawcross waded into the attack that order was restored. The two of them seemed far better able to manage legal niceties that had the other prosecutors floundering. They quickly deflated Goering and Ribbentrop, who followed him, and resumed control.

Hess always remained more than a bit of a mystery to me – in court he was the straight act for Goering with his quips. I often wondered, as

no doubt did many others, just what his aims were when he flew to
Scotland to see the Duke of Hamilton, Scotland's premier Duke. What
passed between them and Churchill we were never told. If we were
prepared to lay our lives on the line, at least they should have had the
grace to tell us and let us decide what was best for us! Rumour had it
that Germany either wanted to sue for peace or wanted Britain to
unite with Germany and fight against the Bolsheviks. I also wondered
why the Russians were subsequently so insistent that he remained in
Spandau prison until he died. At the time I thought that Stalin had believed the latter possibility and that's why they kept him in prison. Ar-
ticles in the press in 1987 which tell of a secret trip by Hess to see Stalin in 1952 at the time the Russians had their spell of guarding
Spandau only makes the business more mysterious. Hess was offered
the leadership of a new German Socialist Party, an offer he apparently
refused.

My assistant duly arrived, a Scots Guardsman, Campbell by name.
He had a shock of black curly hair, narrow craggy features and a broad
Glaswegian accent. I immediately labelled him 'Jock' and we got on
like a house on fire right from the start. He was older than me and had
been in the police force in Glasgow – he was what the Yanks called a
'tough cookie'. It was nice to have someone other than the birds to
chat to, especially as he shared my passion for soccer. We often spent
our free time kicking a battered football around a nearby park. There
were always plenty of German kids hanging around only too ready to
make up a couple of scratch teams. By now it was summer and we
swam in the river that flowed through the park. It was quite deep and
Jock would hold my head up as I splashed around trying to master the
art of swimming. It didn't do to think too much about the colour of
the water – anyone in their right mind wouldn't even have paddled in
it – but it didn't harm us and we had a lot of fun.

While we swam and splashed water over all and sundry the kids
used our uniforms as goal posts. We didn't object. At least they kept
an eye on them for us. It was strange to be in the river among the Germans, stripped of our clothes, and rid of any distinction between us.
Only our language separated us. All the killing seemed pointless and
all the more when you looked at these people enjoying the same innocent pleasures.

The park was a great place for picking up the girls. In the sunny
weather they sunbathed there and, after spotting the ones that took
our fancy we would 'accidently' kick the ball their way and chat them
up when we retrieved it.

A couple of days later I reported to Captain Casson's room for the
day's orders and on being bidden to enter found him on the toilet

again – door wide open in full view. He chatted away completely un-embarrassed and, having completed his toilet, he invited me to sit down and began chatting about this and that, over a drink.

'I've got some photos to show you', he said, producing some snap-shots. I wondered what sort! The snaps were of hotels he owned in Switzerland and other places.

'I can fix you up a job in one of these hotels', he said as he handed them to me one by one. 'He must be loaded', I thought 'or feeling very gay.'

'All very interesting sir', I said, 'but I'm a regular soldier with a long time to serve yet – and it's time I was moving.'

'Why?'

'Well, I've got this girl friend I've promised to meet.'

'A girl?'

'Yes, sir. I can fix you up with one if you like.'

'No thanks, McCarthy, I don't think so.'

And I left him, looking very lonely as he gazed at his holiday snaps on his sofa.

That evening we visited a bar that was very popular with us and the GIs. As the evening wore on we had quite a few drinks, got pally with about a half dozen Yanks and left with them for a dance that was be-ing held in their barracks. As we were walking past the sentry a little horseplay was going on and as I grappled with a GI things got a bit out of control. We started sparring up and belting each other. The rest of the lads crowded round as we pasted each other and one of the Yanks bawled out 'Come on Rocky – Say, Mac, d'you know who you're fight-ing? That's Rocky Graziano!'

'Rocky Graziano?' I thought, as we grabbed each other in a clinch. It dawned on me that I was scrapping with the Middleweight Champion of the World! To the chorus of 'Come on Mac' and the yelling for 'Rocky' we just slugged it out, the pair of us so drunk we could hardly stand, let alone land punches. We both fell to the floor and suddenly became the best of pals – hugging each other round the shoulders as we were hauled to our feet by our mates. I have a vague recollection of sleeping on a pile of crates in the GI canteen that night.

Back at the trials, or the 'Floorshow' as we called it, it was business as usual. The Russian judges were still looking impassive but arguing eve-ry point in their dogmatic way. Goering was blustering and postering in his jodhpurs and black jackboots. Yet another American prosecutor was making a fool of himself questioning Schatts, the financial wizard, on finance. Sandy Birkett peered at the scene over his specs and jotted down points on his notepad. He summed up court proceedings at the end of each day. Lord Justice Lawrence was not missing a thing either, shrewdly weighing up the evidence just as he had weighed me up with the drinking water when I first met him. Dame Laura Knight was still busily painting away in the small studio to the right of the public gallery. The prisoners looked very pensive and some were chatting to their lawyers who represented them, sitting just in front. As I said, business as usual.

The girl friend situation had become a little tricky and I was having to take evasive action. One girl's brother was a waiter at the hotel and I was having to avoid him too as he always seemed to be armed with messages from her arranging yet another date. In short she wanted to make the arrangement permanent and I didn't. Life was getting awkward.

I came in one afternoon to find Jock looking more solemn than usual.

'Do you know Mac, one of the lads has come across this old Scots lady, she lives in Nuremburg in a flat all by herself.'

'That's incredible', I said. 'How did you find out about her?'

'One of the Welsh Guards drivers told me about her just now in the canteen. I've got her address – let's go and visit her.'

'Cor – thats amazin'. She must have been through all that bombing and shelling by the Yanks. When are you planning on goin'?'

'Tomorrow afternoon – about tea time.'

'Right', I said. 'We'll have to get some rations for her from the stores – tea, coffee, and canned meat, that sort of thing. I'd better go down stairs now and grab McCormick before he goes off duty and scrounge some stuff off 'im.'

We skipped down the back stairs and run slap into my persistent girlfriend's brother.

'Can't stop', I shouted as we shot past him, leaving him open-mouthed in mid sentence.

We found McCormick and told him about the Scots woman. 'Bullshit' was his comment.

'Straight up, Gus', I assured him. 'Jock – tell him what you told me.'

Jock started to tell him the tale but was quickly interrupted.

'Can't understand a goddam word you're saying. Pal – say it again slow, fella – you've found a Scotchwoman where?'

'She's livin' by herself here in Nuremburg – she's survived your f...in' bombs and all we want from you, pal, is a tin of coffee and a tin of tea.'

'Well I'll be damned', he croaked. 'Why didn't you say that in the first place?', scratching his balding head. He looked again at the pair of us. 'You're not such a bad sort after all. OK, you've got my permission. Hey Mitchell, see to these guys double sharp.'

'Thank you, sir.'

'Least I could do. Good-luck!', he replied and walked off.

'Right you's guys, whaddaya want? I reckon you could charm the birds off the trees – the way you get round the Colonel – yessir I do declare!', Mitchell chortled as he searched around and found the tea, coffee and a few bits and pieces.

'Put it on some top brass's account', I ordered as he handed the stuff over.

'Say, Mac, would the old lady like some gum?'

'Yeah. Why not?'

He handed us a pack of the stuff that used to make my jaw ache, all that chewing.

'Thanks, Mitch, you're a pal.' I grinned at him and off we went before he could change his mind.

The next afternoon we smartened ourselves up and searched around behind the railway for the tenement block where the old lady lived. Eventually, after having to ask directions from several Germans, we found it – a large, battered block of flats. We climbed the gloomy stone stairs and knocked on the door. After a brief silence there was a shuffling and the door opened enough to reveal a grey haired old lady. Her eyes widened as she saw military uniforms, so we quickly said 'Good Evening'. I left Jock to do the introductions, feeling she would be more at ease with his Scots accent. She asked us in when she heard Jock's voice and soon we were sitting in comfort listening to her story. She said that she had previously had a visit from some Welsh Guards drivers. We handed her the tea, coffee, cans of food and chocolate bars, and as we relaxed in each other's company I asked her how she came to be living there. She told us that after the First World War she had married a German seaman who had brought her back to Germany. He had been killed and she had been left to survive as best as she could. During the worst of the raids on Nuremburg she had taken shelter in the bunkers. She described how terrible it had been, with hundreds killed in widespread devastation. She was a lovely old lady and her pale blue eyes lit up as she listened to Jock's accent – she clasped her hands in enjoyment as they talked about Glasgow and the Clyde. We had a lovely evening, and before we left she insisted on making us a hot drink with the tea we had brought. I gave her a packet of cigarettes which made her raise her eyebrows as she was a non-smoker – but I pointed out that she could buy other things with them and she laughingly accepted them.

This tiny Scots lady became 'granny' to several other Scots Guards over the next few months. Her shabby but spotless flat became a home from home for us.

The situation with Ingrid, the persistent girl friend, had become acutely embarrassing in the meanwhile. I decided to tell her that I was not going to see her again and try to explain why. I told her as gently as I could, for I really didn't want to hurt her. I explained that there could be no future in the relationship and that I didn't want to hurt her, but that she must stop hanging around the hotel waiting for me and that it would be best if we parted. She cried on my shoulder and asked if we could make love one last time. I agreed, after checking that I had the necessary rubber goods, and we found a nice spot under some trees and did just that. I felt lousy about packing her up, but I really couldn't cope with a long-term relationship.

After a tearful farewell on Ingrid's part I walked back to the Grand Hotel and found pandemonium there. A Russian officer had been shot and had staggered into the hotel where he collapsed on the plush carpet of the foyer and died, his blood leaving a rusty red stain. People came running out of the dining room to see what the commotion was all about. There were MPs everywhere and some Russians had arrived from somewhere and were busy putting the body on a stretcher. They whisked him away at high speed. All the time this high drama was taking place in the foyer the band in the marble room played on as if nothing had happened. The tell-tale sign of blood on the carpet was very evident, though the shooting was a mystery. Nobody knew who had shot the bloke and the Ruskies weren't saying anything. The staff cleaned up the blood stains with their usual efficiency, and life quickly returned to normal.

One of the nicer parts of hotel life was our easy going relationships with the room maids. There were several of them and the one who made our beds was a particularly pretty girl. I never made it with her – not for the want of trying, mind you. I got pretty close one evening when she invited me to her room, which was on the floor below and on the other side of the building. One evening I told Jock I was going to see if the bathroom was free.

'Oh yeah – at 11p.m.?' he retorted, knowing bloody well where I was going.

I had all the directions and set off to find her room. I went into the room, slipping in quietly in my socks and calling her name softly as I shut the door behind me. I located the bed in the dark and touched the body in the bed, whispering 'Ziggy'.

A startled Frenchman sat up in bed and his wife in the other bed started shouting in alarm. Stupidly I just stood there in the dark saying 'You're not Ziggy.'"

'Ziggy?', queried the alarmed Frenchman.

'Mon dieu', wailed the Frenchwoman.

'Sorry – I'm looking for Ziggy', I explained as I beat a hasty and embarrassed retreat from their room, hoping to get clear before the Frenchwoman started hollering any louder. Red faced I stood outside cursing my luck. I fumed and started out once more to find Ziggy's room. Eventually I found the right room, this time calling her name from the door in case I had made another mistake. There was movement from the bed and a lamp switched on revealing two single beds – Ziggy in one and another girl in the other bed.

'What do you want?', whispered Ziggy, recognising me.

'I've come to make love to you, but not to an audience, honey', I replied and turned and walked out again. I gave up, completely put off – and as I crept back to my bed reflected that I couldn't win them all. Jock was surprised to see me back so soon. 'You were quick', he commented.

'Not really – didn't even get started'. I told him what had happened and he laughed his head off.

My luck really wasn't any better the next night. I had returned late one evening to the hotel quite drunk after a long evening in a beer cellar, drinking and listening to a glamorous girl singing 'Sentimental Journey'. I and the rest of the GIs suddenly felt homesick. It was the way she sang, soft and sultry like – and boy did it register!

I wanted to check the register for VIP arrivals and departures and had to queue behind a couple of American women wanting their room keys. They, too, were quite drunk and looked as if they had had a good evening. 'Fritz' the receptionist asked me if I would see them to their rooms, which I duly did. We were all very drunk and before I knew it they had undressed and climbed into separate beds and I climbed into the bed of the last one to get undressed. Force of habit, I suppose. The trouble was I was still dressed and I had to climb out again and struggle out of my army blouse and trousers armed with a french letter in one hand. I couldn't extract it from its wrapper either and while I was thus engaged the woman started talking to me, telling about her daughter! 'Just about your age', she assured me. 'By the way, what are you doing?', she asked, as I finally got back into her bed.

'I'm trying to make love to you.'

'Oh', she said and rolled onto her back. Seeing the french letter in place, she proceeded to remove it.

'Can't abide rubber', she said, dropping it over the side of the bed. I tried to make love to her but by now I had gone off the boil and only succeeded in rolling off her and promptly falling asleep. When I awoke early next morning she had obviously had enough of my company and had moved into the other bed with her friend. I had her bed to myself and for a minute had no idea where I was. When it dawned on me I thought I'd better clear out, and collecting my boots, tunic and trousers tiptoed in my underpants along the hotel corridor, carrying the uniform in my arms up the back stairs into my own bed.

A few hours later I was busy and ran into her in the hotel doorway. I don't know which of the two of us was the more embarrassed.

I was doing really well on the black market. I used to set out the stuff for sale on the beds and the customers would queue in the doorway, controlled by Jock. The money I earned far exceeded my pay, which I didn't bother drawing for months on end. At one point I decided I'd better open a bank account and went to the German bank along the High Street. They were very suspicious, and the language difficulties didn't help, nor did the fact that I gave my address as the Grand Hotel. I wished I'd had Rosie with me, I thought, she would have sorted it out – I needed her right there and then, I mused. They gave me a whole sheaf of forms to fill in and told me to return the next day with them completed. Suddenly it didn't seem to be such a good idea. Armed with the forms I walked back to the hotel and ran into Cox and Renfrew, my two GI mates.

'We've been looking for you Mac', said Cox. 'How do you fancy ... How do you fancy a trip down to Munich tomorrow? We've managed to get hold of a jeep for the day. How about asking Jock, too, and we'll make a foursome.'

'Yeah, fine, so long as he doesn't bring his bag-pipes with 'im', I replied.

I returned to our room, found Jock and told him the plans. He was delighted.

Early next morning Cox and Renfrew, both spotless and in their best service dress (what else, when they ran the hotel's dry-cleaning department?) turned up with a jeep. Not to be outdone Jock and I also had our best uniform on and our brass and leather polished until they gleamed. Cox, the driver, let out a loud 'Yahoo' and we squealed our way over the cobbles heading for Munich. Grabbing our caps before they could be blown off we settled down to enjoy the journey.

The drive was magic – it was good to be away from all the dereliction of the towns and out in the fresh air. Munich was very busy, full of military traffic and personnel, and we were stopped at one point by an American Military policeman and told to pull over to the side. Cox had to explain what we were doing. We drove on, pulled up outside the American Red Cross and hopped into their parlour for coffee and donuts, magnificent and free, served to us by women dressed in brown uniforms with the Red Cross insignia. The British had nothing similar – the NAAFI charged you for everything.

After seeing the sights and having a jar or two in the beer cellars we got talking about Garmisch Partenkirken – a mecca for touring American service men and women. It wasn't far away but after thinking about it we decided the visit would have to wait as we really didn't have the time. It was late when we finally set off back to Nuremburg, praying that we didn't get a puncture on the way. It had been a great day.

Back in the hotel a couple of days later I ran into my old mate from Zirndorf, the manager of the football team and one of the pool of drivers.

'I've got a "jam jar" outside – it's that long black limmo', he said. I looked out through the window at the shining black car parked outside the front of the hotel. 'Looks like a Packard', I said.

'Tisn't – it's bullet proof though.'

'You're kiddin!'

'I'll take you to Furth and back – mind yer fingers', and he slammed the heavy door shut.

The car was huge – enough room in the back to hold an electric organ. I sat back and enjoyed the luxury of real leather upholstery and the muted sound of traffic as we sped along the road to Furth. When we arrived Tubby pulled over and came round to the back door and opened it.

'What do you think?'

'Smashin, the traffic sounds quieter than when yer on the jeeps.' Tubby looked puzzled and glanced at the door.

'You've 'ad the bleedin window rolled down in a bullet proof car you stoopid sod.' He rolled up the window and as he shut the door once more said 'Right, we'll try it again.'

This time it was absolutely silent in the car – no sound of traffic, nothing – a funny, almost claustrophobic experience. I could see Tubby's grinning face in the driving mirror as he watched my reactions.

When we arrived outside the Palace Courthouse we had a good look at the car – it was made of steel, very much thicker than the normal type, and the windows were of bullet proof glass – again much thicker than normal. Tubby told me it was only used for special occasions, so whoever he delivered to the Courthouse that day must have been someone very important.

The British prosecutors were having a field day in the court room. They were presenting damning evidence against Keitel and Goering in the form of signed instructions for the murder of some of the RAF boys who had escaped from a POW camp. Most had been murdered and very few escaped to tell the awful story. Sir Hartley Shawcross and Sir David Maxwell-Fyffe, our two main prosecutors, pressed home their attacks as Goering and Keitel squirmed in the dock. Later, when films of the concentration camps were shown, several of the prisoners refused to watch them, simply staring ahead with deadpan faces. An unnatural hush was felt in the gallery as people around me couldn't believe what they were seeing as the film unfolded the truth.

9

Two Tales of Two Cities

Jock found me one afternoon with a message that I was to return to Zirndorf to replace Bill, who was going on leave. They were sending transport for me the next morning. I telephoned Rosie to give her this news. I had made a date with her, which I had been looking forward to and I was now cancelling it much to our regret. I would be even further away from her now it seemed. After saying my farewells to Jock, Fritz, Cox and Renfrew, I waved, and made my way back to the foyer where I waited for the transport.

'Wotcha mate.' I greeted the driver when he eventually turned up, 'Got one of those nice Humber Snipe staff cars outside?'

'Take a gander, Mac.'

I looked through the entrance doors.

'A bleedin jeep', I expostulated. 'What if it rains!'

'We'll stop under a tree.'

'Oh very funny', I retorted, and we both laughed.

I was quite sad to leave the Grand Hotel. There was always something going on and I enjoyed being in the centre of things. I hoped that it would be restored to its former glory. I did hear that Hitler was refused a room there once, before he became the Fuehrer, because they thought him a trouble maker. Later he had had a special suite of rooms created so that he could stay there when he liked.

It was a pleasant drive back; the trees were on the turn and the river meandered its course just below the road. I hoped Bill would get back safely for a well earned rest. I dumped my kit-bag in his room and made a tour of inspection. I checked the brewing up facilities and then had a good look over my lovely Opel car, which Bill had been looking after for me. It really was a bit of a white elephant, for I couldn't get petrol for it. I even thought about trying to get it back to Blighty but it would have to be disguised as an American staff car if I was to succeed. All I needed was a white star and a coat of camouflage-coloured paint. Other people 'acquired' more easily transported and hidden commodities like jewellery and oil paintings which were resold in Britain. I often thought about that lovely oil painting above the Lawrence's bed in Stielen Strasse, but I imagine he and his missus would have something to say if it went missing. Regretfully I decided I would have to sell the car. I knew Hans, our stoker at Lindenhof, would know where to get a good price. I told him I wanted 250 Reichmarks or 100 cigarettes for it. He raised his eyebrows but said he would see what he could do.

Major Airey Neave and a civilian were billeted at the house and my job was to look after them. Unlike the Grand Hotel the laundry system at Zirndorf left much to be desired and I was always chasing the housekeeper to find out what had happened to Major Neave's underwear. At the start of the trials his job had been to read out the indictments to all the prisoners in their cells, and he sat in court on the secretaries' bench to the left of the judges.

One evening the major told me that his wife was coming for a visit so I gave instructions to the hausfrau to put flowers round the place and generally prepare for her visit by polishing a bit harder and getting the washing back faster. On the morning after her arrival I took tea to them, leaving it on the bedside table on her side. She was pretty, with, if I remember rightly, a shock of brown curls.

It was nice to see Fred again – he'd soon turned up when he heard I was back.

'How's ol' Harry? Where is he?' I wanted to know.

'Gone back to Blighty', said Fred. ''E's left a message for yer -- Don't shag the kitchen maid – 'e caught a dose of the clap from her.'

'Poor ol' sod – fancy that! Anyway – how's your love life Fred – any progress with your lady friend?'

'No – had a row with the old man about it – he's complaining about the paper work and whatever.'

'Can't you just bugger off to a German registry office and get married?'

'I wish I could', he said glumly.

'Is the rest of my gear still safe in the attic?' I wanted to know – I seemed to have stuff stored up all around Zirndorf.

'Yeah – sure Mac', Fred assured me.

We walked over to Lindenhof where there was a barrel of beer for the officers' use in the lounge. Everyone was out at the trials so we settled down in the lounge with beer and fags. We hadn't been there long before Hans, the stoker, knocked on the door and came in with a fistful of Reichmark notes. He had sold the car. I counted the money, watched closely by Fred, and told Hans he could have his cut in money or fags – he opted for 20 Lucky Strikes.

Fred laughed as Hans left the room 'How much did you make on that little transaction?'

'Work it out for yourself', I replied, as I pushed the wad of notes into my breast pocket. 'It cost me 20 ciggies and I sold it for 250 Reichmarks.'

'Not bad, not bad', says Fred. 'With all that money, how about being my best man?'

I looked at him dumfounded. 'No Fred. Not again mate!' I still had painful memories of the last time.

Life was much slower at Zirndorf and time hung on our hands. The trials were coming to a climax and everyone was at the courtroom during the day. We passed the time in the cafe, cinema or just chatting up the birds. I met one particularly gorgeous girl and spent an afternoon with her and her father near the woods sitting and drinking beer outside an Inn. I tried my best to get her to bed but she had a GI Joe lined up and I never got anywhere. Some you win, some you lose.

For a few weeks past the leg that I bashed up some time before had been playing up and it was now getting really painful. The skin was becoming ulcerated where it had been damaged and the wounds were getting larger. I thought it about time I did something about it.

We had no doctor in the village so I cadged a lift to the American Army hospital where I had been treated for the original injuries. The doctor who saw me diagnosed ulcers and insisted on keeping me in so that they could treat me properly. A blood sample and form-filling session later, I found myself in a bed in a small ward with five GIs. Having settled myself in the corner of the room I looked about me and was puzzled to see a guard on duty inside the ward, near the door. He was carrying a .45 revolver. I wondered about my fellow inmates and what they had been up to.

The next morning the usual gaggle of doctors and nurses did their rounds and looked me over – later I was given 'medication' as they called it and my leg was dressed. My temperature and pulse were recorded on the chart at the bottom of the bed.

I had plenty of time now to look at my fellow patients. They looked a hard lot – one of them was the spitting image of Humphrey Bogart, with all his mannerisms and even the same scar. He came over after a while.

'You're a Limey ain't yer, pal?'

'Sure thing fella', I replied.

He pulled long and hard on a fag with his eyes narrowed against the smoke – just like Humph.

By now another armed guard had been posted – this one also in the ward. He stood impassively behind 'Humph' listening to every word, his eyes glinting under his helmet. I couldn't work out *why* there were so many guards around this part of the hospital; I got the impression that these guys were from the stockade.

Over the next few days I had several blood tests and dressings. I was told to rest the leg, so I spent hours on my bed watching the scene. The other lads played cards by the hour. I couldn't join in because the game they played was strange to me – it was poker – but slowly I picked it up as it was a bit like brag, a game we had played in the Bunk. Eventually I felt competent enough to play when they invited me one evening. I played it cagey still, though.

'How d'yer play the game?', I asked innocently, as I took my place round the table.

'I'll show yer kiddo – just you watch me.'

'What are the stakes?'

'Butts, cigarettes'. He introduced me to the school: 'This is Billy, that's George, over there is Fuzzy and I'm Larry. We'll play a dummy hand. You'll get the idea.'

'OK. Deal me in'

'What's yer name, boy – we can't just keep calling yer Limey.'

'Call me Mac.'

That evening I lost left, right and centre, so I dropped out and just watched – picking up pointers and learning fast.

When the doctors came round the next morning they expressed satisfaction with my leg – it was healing and certainly felt more comfortable. I spent the afternoon reading a book from the mobile trolley. At one point I hopped along to the lavatory down the corridor, accidently bumping into an American nurse and her friends.

'You're the Limey aren't you?', she enquired.

'Yes I am', I replied.

'Get a load of his accent girls', she called to her friends. They gathered round and I spent an embarrassing few minutes repeating the word 'bottle' for them – they were fascinated.

At last I got back to the room, where I found the poker players waiting for me.

'Here's the son of a gun – come on Mac, we're waiting for you.'

'Alright, lads – what's the stakes?'

'Money. Bucks, greenbacks.'

'Money?' I got this feeling in the back of my neck that they thought they were going to make easy pickings off me.

'Yes – money.'

'Right – count me in.'

It was one of those all too rare days when everything goes your way. I won the first two hands and my confidence grew – I had got the idea of the game. I won several more hands. I could do nothing wrong!

'Limey – could you lend me a few bucks?', asked Larry, after a while.

'Sure – how much d'you want? And the name's Mac', I replied, holding a fistful of dollars in my mitt.

'About 5 bucks.'

'Here y'are fella – cop hold of those' and I handed him the script coupons that represented money.

All of a sudden 'the Limey' had become money lender to the US Armed Forces! The room became very quiet and tense and the words 'Jesus Christ' were very evident through the smoke of Camel cigarettes. Still I could not put a foot wrong and a couple of hours later I had cleaned them out!

'I'll pay you the end of the week, you lucky son of a bitch', promised Larry, as we stood up and stretched after the session.

'Yeah – I know you will, Larry – there's no problem fella', I replied.

Next evening they were playing with IOUs and still the guards were there – one at each end of the room. This time they were talking and arguing across the room while we were sitting between them trying to concentrate. The arguing had developed into a shouting match and when I heard one of them shout 'I can beat you to the draw anytime, soldier', I froze.

'Yeah, moonface, just let's try it', yelled the other sentry, and the card school froze. We looked at each other and then at the two guards, who by then had unbuttoned their holsters and were preparing to draw. The card game stopped and we sat there not even breathing – it was like 'High Noon'. You could almost see the tension.

The two soldiers went for their guns and we dived for the floor. Larry shouted out, 'You crazy sons of a bitch. What the shit are you guys up to – you trigger happy cock suckers. This is a goddam hospital not a f...... John Wayne movie!'

This seemed to stop them in their tracks, but their hands continued to hover around their holsters. Larry was the first to get up off the floor and he was furious.

'We've had enough of you bullshitting around in here', he fumed. 'I'm going for the MO.' He stormed out of the room, flinging the door open so violently that it crashed against the wall. Soon he returned with the MO.

'What's going on here?', he demanded. We told him.

'We want these two punks outside the room – we can't sleep knowing they're in here likely to plug us with their .45s', Larry stormed. He was still mad – understandably – and he voiced what was in all our minds. 'We want them out NOW.'

The MO digested Larry's forcefully put comments. Eventually the two guards were escorted out by some of the other officers who had come to see what the commotion was about. Another guard was posted in the ward and another outside the door.

'This goddam place is SNAFU' (situation normal all fouled up) shouted Larry, as he punched the wall with his fist. But after a while life returned to normal. The poker game resumed, but I had had enough and declined their invitation to rejoin them.

True to their word, each of them paid me what they owed at the end of the week. My leg was also on the mend and I was able to walk on it, albeit very gently and very slowly. They reckoned another week of treatment and rest and I would be able to return to Zirndorf.

After a couple of weeks in hospital I was pronounced fit and discharged. I got a lift back in an American army meat waggon and reported to the old man. All the time I was there I only once had a visit – Jughead my Cornish wrestler mate had come in early on – and this puzzled me until the colonel opened his mouth. He said that they would have visited me but they thought it was a VD hospital and that they hadn't liked to be seen visiting that kind of establishment. He was sure I understood – but I didn't! Compared with people like the colonel, the rough, tough bunch of GI lads I had spent the past couple of weeks with were like a breath of fresh air. They were honest and they cared about each other – they had been a smashing set of mates.

I had been worried about my leg and made up my mind that I would strictly ration the booze and women and get myself really fit. I started training sessions down at the gymnasium and took long runs around the countryside. I became a fitness freak. And I was amazed how beautiful the countryside was – it was Autumn and the leaves on the trees were golden as I ran in a large circle around the village. Men were working in the fields and flocks of birds followed the horse-drawn ploughs. Sometimes kids would run along with me for a while trying to keep up. My circular route took me past the underground bunkers in the woods and I again wondered what secrets they hid. Sometimes I joined the kids on the village green as they kicked around an ancient battered leather football that had seen more stitches than any Brighton razor gang.

Meanwhile, despite all the arguments, obstructions and delaying tactics by the defence counsels and the Russians, the trials were reaching the stage where judgement would be pronounced and sentence passed. As this time drew closer, so security became all the more intense. Sherman tanks were rumbled into position around the Palace and bullet-proof cars were used to ferry the judges to and fro. GIs stood behind sandbags with their automatic weapons at the ready. Almost overnight the area around Furtherstrasse where the courthouse stood had become a fortress.

All the evidence had been presented and the arguments given and in the underground cells adjoining the courthouse the Nazi prisoners awaited judgement. For a while there was fierce opposition from the Russians to the acquittal of Schatz, Fritze and Von Papen – they demanded death for the lot, Stalin's orders. After the judges had adjourned the trials for a period in order to sum up, the day of judgement arrived. The prisoners were led out to learn their fate. One at a time they were escorted to the dock by the 'snowdrops' to face the president of the International Military Tribunal, Lord Justice Lawrence, who pronounced sentence, then they were escorted back to their bench, some congratulating each other on their acquittal, others returning under the sentence of death.

Goering was sentenced to death on four counts. He asked if he could be shot, rather than hanged, as a military man, but this was refused, which seemed unreasonable to me. As it was he escaped hanging by taking a cyanide pill and dying by his own hand. Rumour had it that one of the German trustees had smuggled it in for him.

Hess was sentenced to life imprisonment on two counts. He committed suicide in strange circumstances in 1987 despite the vigilance of the Americans whose turn it was to guard Spandau at the time of his lonely demise. Ribbentrop, Keitel, Rosenburg, Saukel, Seyss-Inquart were all sentenced to death on four counts; Frank, Frick and Johdl were to die on three counts each. Kaltenbrunner was to die on two counts and Striecher, the 'Jew baiter', on one count. Funk and Raeder got life imprisonment, Von Shirach and Speer got 20 years apiece, Neurath got 15 years and Doenitz got 10. Martin Bormann, Hitler's deputy, was sentenced to death on four counts in his absence.

So the most famous trial in history came to an end. After last rites were given to them, they were hanged in a Gymnasium by an American, Master Sergeant Woods, who was the official executioner for the US Armed Forces, in the early hours of an October morning. Journalists who were present commented on the bungled job that was made. It was claimed that one was left gurgling and writhing while others hit their faces on the end of the platform because the rope was the wrong length – charges that were strongly denied by the Americans. It was also said that one of them shouted 'One day the Russians will do this to you' and another 'Long Live Germany.' Goering had said 'The conquerors would always vanquish the victims' before he died, but he didn't have the press present at the time.

Afterwards the bodies were taken away secretly to a place south of Munich where they were cremated and their ashes disposed of.

It seemed unfair to me at the time that the banker should be there in court while Krupp – the bloke responsible for all the munition manufactured – escaped being tried on grounds of ill health. Yet ten years later Krupp's industrial empire was once again in full swing.

With the end of the trial in sight, talk of going home spread among the GIs. Poor old Fred was still trying to get permission to marry his German girl, while so many GIs had married local women that they had to queue up to get home. The ships were packed with servicemen and their German wives.

I was given leave too, as the judges had now done their jobs and were returning home. Several of us made our preparations for leave and joined the train for Paris from the Central Station at Nuremburg. We had to stand, as the train was already full when it pulled in. Many were refugees escaping from the Russians, with only what they stood up in. The train seemed to rumble on for ever – stopping in the middle of nowhere for hours on end, then suddenly jerking and clanking into life again to go a few more miles. We sat on our kit-bags in the corridor and smoked, joked and laughed. Some of us played cards to pass the time. The married men among us voiced the hope that the milkman hadn't been knocking too often.

I had picked up enough German to carry on conversations with German speaking passengers, swapping cigs for black bread and smelly sausage. When we got stiff it was almost a pleasure to stretch our legs along the corridor – stepping over sleeping bodies, piles of luggage and equipment. Just before the French border a po-faced ticket collector checked our papers without comment. You could see several people noticeably relax as we crossed the border into France. I assumed they were refugees or escaping POWs, but they weren't about to confirm or deny my assumptions.

At Bar-le-Duc the train stopped. I was desperate to get to the lavatory. I asked a passing official how long we'd be there and he replied about 20 minutes. I made a beeline for the Gents and dropping my trousers sat on a wooden plank and let rip. I glanced to my right and saw to my considerable surprise a woman doing exactly the same at the other end of the plank! I couldn't believe it! When I got back to the train I told the lads and there was a sudden rush for the bogs!

We arrived in Paris tired and starving hungry – to be told that we had to make our own way to Pigalle, where we were to stay in a transit camp. The 'camp' turned out to be a long room above a garage. There seemed to be some delay at the Channel ports and we were told we were to stay until this problem was sorted out. Our hearts sank at this news – transit camps were grubby and uncomfortable in our experience, and this one turned out to be no exception.

We had bunk beds in a cold room with filthy windows which overlooked the fire-escape-festooned backs of buildings opposite. The whole building was seedy and run down and in dire need of a bloody good clean from top to bottom. I was dozing on a top bunk when there was a commotion from one of the windows, wolf whistles and cheers and yells of 'Take 'em off.' I went over to see what was going on, climbing onto another top bunk to see as there was such a crush at the window. There on the fire escape opposite was a woman showing all she'd got to us, while on the floor below another bird was busy blowing up french letters like ballons. They were obviously prostitutes and each one was trying to outdo the other. A cheer that a Wembley crowd would have envied greeted the one who dropped her knickers and wiggled her bare arse at us. There was pandemonium. Some of the lads were breathing on the windows and writing messages on them like 'Tonight', 'How much?', 'Do you take Reichmarks?'. It was a pimp's paradise. We were treated to two shows daily – one in the morning and the other we called 'Evening in Paris'. I hadn't seen the lads so excited since the first night we delivered the girls in the Bahnhof Express.

I was too tired and hungry to feel tempted and decided to go for a stroll and try to get some grub. I didn't stray too far, as I didn't want to get lost in the jungle of newly liberated Paris. Pigalle was full of life and flashing lights, making it hard to remember there had been a war. There were a lot of GIs milling about, hanging around the amusement arcades and cafes and picking up the girls. I enjoyed an hour or so playing the pinball machines and just looking at the lights – they made me long for the Piccadilly I had known before the war, before the lights went out.

The main street of Pigalle was a series of cafes and knocking shops – I got approached more times that evening than you would believe. They were offering two girls for the price of one – I thought I was dreaming! A lone GI heard the offer and asked if he could take one off my hands. 'Yeah? Swell buddie – why not?', I said.

'Lets go kid' and up the sleazy stairs we clattered. It smelt nothing like Covent Garden on a spring morning in Floral Hall – not even much like a high class brothel in Mayfair. But the blood was up and we weren't too particular.

'Say bud – give me a call when you've finished pal.'

'Sure thing Yank', I replied as we parted company. And in no time it was over and we were sitting up smoking.

I got dressed and called for the Yank. 'You OK there, bud?'

'Sure thing, Mac – just leave me to die in "Gay Paree" – I've got me dog-tags and I wanner stay with this broad – I'm coming up for the third time!'

'O.K. buster. It's your funeral – watch out for the cops or the "redcoats" you lucky son of a bitch – so long pal!'

Hanging on to the bannisters for support I clattered down the steep staircase and out into the street where I took several deep breaths to clear my nostrils. I pointed my nose down a side street and walked down one side and up the other.

Paris was a hell of a place to be right then, it was full of pick-pockets, pimps, money sharks and every kind of two-bit punk you could rake up. Trouble and violence flared with monotonous regularity in the sleazy joints and dark back streets. I had seen many fights in my life and had been involved in some but the one that took the cake started later that night next to me in an amusement arcade while I was playing a pinball machine. For a while I was worried they would tilt the machine but they moved away, fought and kicked the length of the arcade and ended up in the middle of Pigalle itself before the MPs arrived and carted them away – blood everywhere, both bruised and battered and barely recognisable.

I felt shattered as I drew close to the garage-cum-transit camp that first night and jokingly thought 'What I need is a new piston and a decoke.'

A couple of the lads were standing in the entrance of the garage as I arrived, and they asked me if anything exciting was going on out there. 'Nah – pretty tame, fellas', I replied with a straight face. They looked closely and noticed a gleam in my eye – but fancy standing there and asking questions when they had a chance to see for themselves.

The transit camp was only half full and we could spread out a bit, but nobody wanted to stay there a minute longer than was necessary. After the mannequin parade on the fire escape stairs a few mornings later, we cornered the leader and demanded information. We'd been there five days and the poor sod was getting it in the neck because of some seamen's strike at the Channel ports. There was talk of flying us out but nothing came of that plan. The longer we were there the more acute our cash flow problems became and fewer our options for entertainment. I didn't mind being there too much – as a city lad I was very soon at home – but the country lads found it expensive and daunting among the sharks. After a couple weeks of being in the place, though, even the magic of the twice daily show on the fire escapes lost its appeal and the displays no longer drew a full house. It wasn't the kind of place that you wanted to hang about in, but as the cash ran out that was all some of the lads could do.

As I explored the city I began to compare it with London and Nuremburg, but Paris hadn't suffered the physical damage that the British and German cities had. My own beloved city had lost so much in human and historic terms. The wonderful Wren and Hawksmoor churches, the old guild halls and people's homes – not to mention the thousands of lives. Paris had only a few bullet holes – its cost had been in human terms, as the plaques on the street corners gave testimony. The resistance workers had lost their lives on the streets of Paris while General de Gaulle lorded it in the safety of his apartment in Dolphin Square in Pimlico.

Just as we began to despair of ever getting away, we were told to pack and get to the Gare du Nord for a boat train. The glum faces were lit up with grins again and the corny repartee started up – we were actually going to get to dear ol' Blighty.

After an age we were on the Channel and there wasn't a dry eye in the place as the white cliffs of Dover loomed close. I looked for the blue birds in the sky but only saw gulls. The customs had a field day going through our kit-bags, but finally we were on the last leg of our journey. Most of the lads had still more trains to catch, and there were only two of us bound just for London. We arranged to meet under the clock at Victoria for our return journey and went our different ways.

It was strange but great to be back in the Smoke again. As I waited for the tube to Archway and home, my mind went back to the time Dad had carried my kit-bag down to Finsbury Park tube. I hadn't wanted him to but he had insisted. I'd left him at the station entrance close to tears. Now I emerged into daylight at Archway and was soon climbing the stone stairs up to our flat. I pulled the key through the letterbox on its bit of string and let myself in, wondering what had been happening since I was last there. 'I'm back', I shouted, dumping my kit bag in the hall. Mum came out of the kitchen at the sound of my voice.

'Good Lord. What a turn up for the books!', she said, with a wide grin of welcome. 'Have you had anythin' to eat?' Then looking closely at me with those shrewd eyes of hers, she said 'You look baggy round the eyes, Boysie. 'Aven't you bin sleepin' well?'

'Sure, Mum, like a top. I'm starvin'.' Mum made me a cuppa and a thick sandwich while I put my gear away in the small bedroom that I shared with Patsy, my brother.

I demolished the sandwich and sat and talked a while. I asked what time the pubs opened. 'I've got a lot of practice to put in', I joked. I handed her my food coupon too, as food rationing was still in force. It was still like wartime as far as food was concerned – the only difference was the absence of bombs and blackout. There was another difference around the Archway too – the postwar influx of Irish men to clear the bombed sites and Irish girls to staff the hospitals.

I had a great leave, but my leg began to play up again. The ulcers had returned with a vengeance. Matters got so bad that I thought I had better do something about them quick, so I limped to the Military

Hospital at Millbank. After inspecting my leg at length, the doctor there sent me up to one of the wards where I remained for a week. I didn't seem to be getting better so I was told that I was being transferred to the Royal Herbert Hospital at Woolwich where I could get specialist treatment.

At first I was told to make my own way there, but as I was collecting my bits and pieces together I heard a fierce argument outside in the corridor. I was then told to wait as an Army ambulance was going to take me. I sat down to wait. Eventually the ambulance arrived and soon I was on my way to Woolwich, on the other side of London. I passed the time on the journey chatting to the ATS driver who told me that the sister in charge of the ward had hit the roof when she heard that I was expected to make my own way there. She had argued that I was in danger of losing my leg if it didn't heal and that walking all the way across London was just not on. Only then had the ambulance been laid on for me. I was relieved to get away from the stiff and starchy atmosphere of Millbank, although it offered a superb view of the Thames. I was also very shaken to hear just how serious my leg ulcers were.

When I arrived at the Royal Herbert I was escorted to a large ward packed with beds and shown my bed, one in a row down the centre of the ward. A little while later a pretty young nurse arrived to dress my leg. I had on a pair of pyjamas several sizes too large and as I rolled up my trouser leg for her my wedding tackle slipped out from the unbuttoned fly; I was embarrassed and blushed, but she just carried on dressing my leg with a demure smile on her face – she'd seen it all before. I felt lousy and was very depressed about my leg. I nodded off and slept like a log until I was woken next morning.

During the morning some men were discharged and I was transferred to a bed against the wall, which was much better as I could now see what was going on. In the afternoon some ATS girls came in to visit a friend and one of them came over and sat on my bed. 'I'm glad to see you're still alive', she said smiling.

'Sorry?', I said, puzzled.

'Last night you looked as if you were a goner', she explained. 'You looked so white and still in your bed we thought you were on your way out. I'm glad you're not.'

'So'm I!', I replied with feeling, and I laughed. She did too, but her eyes still looked concerned. She bunged me some sweets and said she'd be back on Thursday and would pop over and see me then. She told me she was stationed in the Royal Artillery barracks nearby.

Suddenly I began to feel much better.

My leg was now receiving intensive treatment and I did exactly as I was told and rested it – I didn't want to be minus a leg! I passed the time watching the other blokes in the ward and chatting to those nearby. On the other side of the room were a couple of blokes back from the Burma jungle, a cheerful pair who still wore their wide brimmed bush-hats, but physically they were an awful mess. They were covered with jungle sores and both had beri-beri. They were the lucky ones, they maintained – hundreds of their mates didn't survive.

We passed the time reading newspapers, listening to the wireless, playing housey-housey or tombola or cards. I think I once won 9d. Every evening a bloke came round with the evening papers and one evening he asked me if I would deliver the papers round the wards for him.

'I dunno abaht that, mate', I said. 'How do yer know you can trust me?'

'How?', he replied, looking me straight in the eye. 'Because yer clean shaven, that's why.' To him being clean shaven meant you were an honest bloke. I had to decline though, as I was forbidden to get out of bed and I was hell bent on getting my leg right again. I was obeying orders for a change.

At lights out, the square shouldered figure of the ward sister did a round of inspection to see that everything was in apple pie order. Her uniform crackled with starch and her beady eyes missed nothing. On this particular evening she had just approached the bed opposite mine on the other side of the ward when her booming voice rang out.

'Get your hands out and stop playing about with yourself', she shouted at the poor bloke in the bed.

'My gawd, what a dragon!', I thought, making sure, as we all did, that our hands were where she could see them!

Life took on a routine, broken by meals which weren't too bad if you shut your eyes and pretended you were eating something else. After what seemed years my leg really healed and after a final visit from a specialist I was pronounced fit and discharged.

I returned home and the next morning reported to BWCE to see what was what and get instructions for travelling back to Nuremburg. I approached the two policemen in the entrance hall and signed in before reporting to an office on the first floor. This time a woman was in charge. I introduced myself and explained the circumstances before asking her how I was going to get back to Nuremburg. She silently looked me up and down before going over to a filing cabinet and getting out my file. After a minute or so she told me that every one was moving out from Zirndorf and Nuremburg and that I wouldn't be going back! I was thunderstruck, especially when I remembered all the black market goods I'd stored in the attic together with the rest of my military equipment. I dimly heard her say, 'You will have to report to Windsor.'

'Pardon, madam?'

'Report to Windsor – Victoria Barracks.'

'Victoria Barracks?'

'Yes – Victoria Barracks.'

'Thank you ahem Miss, ahem M'am – Thank you'

'Report in two days time', she ordered.

'Yes, ma'am.'

I nodded to the two policemen in the lobby and stepped out into the square stunned. Victoria Barracks – of all places! That's where I'd started!

Walking through Belgravia for the bus home I spotted a pub and decided that I needed a drink. As I sat in the corner with my pint I reflected on the events and experiences of the past couple of years. It dawned on me that I had been part of, and witness to, a unique historic event. A kid from the Bunk, I had witnessed the most famous trial in history and had seen the Nazi leaders in person. It also occurred to me that although many of the Nazis had been brought to justice and had paid the ultimate price, there were others who had escaped retribution.

I have since come to the conclusion that the trials were little more than a victors' ritual, a salve for the consciences of the Allies. Time has shown that none of the powers involved in the war had clear consciences – each had, to a greater or lesser degree, indulged in their own brand of terror and repression to defend their ideals. Time also heals and dims the memory and these evils are forgotten by most of us. Only a few zealots still hunt for the guilty ones at large.

I savoured the cool beer whilst I pondered on my own future. After the free and easy lifestyle I had enjoyed in Nuremburg I wasn't looking forward to being a peacetime soldier in postwar Britain on 2/- a day. Nor was I looking forward to returning to the stiff discipline of life at Victoria Barracks.

I finished my pint and left the pub somewhat depressed – this and an overwhelming sense of anti-climax stayed with me for a few weeks.

My first day back at Windsor only increased my mood of depression. It was a calamity. When I tried to get some pay from the acquittance roll (a substitute pay list), the young officer looked me up and down and asked me when I had last had a haircut. I told him about thirty minutes ago, which was true, but I had bunged the barber to give me a decent cut. This chico wasn't satisfied, however, and I was escorted back and back again to get more taken off. Three haircuts in one day! I looked like a convict. I was well and truly back to the old unchanging routine of the Brigade of Guards. The trouble now was that I had changed. I was no longer in the mood to be messed about by youngsters still wet behind the ears.

The new intake were much younger and very soon I came to be regarded as the 'elder statesman' of the barrack room, constantly asked for my opinion on all manner of things. I was missing my mates – I never did see any of them again – and I hated the routine. I did more than my share of punishments for the lack of the right gear and my refusal to knuckle down. I fought much of my aggression off in the boxing ring, representing my platoon, getting bloody noses and black eyes for my pains.

All around me the men who had been called up were being demobbed and were returning to their wives and families, while I, an army regular, had to soldier on. I remained unsure of my future – wanting to get abroad again yet lacking the motivation and idealism that had led me to volunteer. Peacetime had brought its own crop of problems for me. What was my role to be as a soldier now? I no longer saw life in black and white. I was now aware that it was in reality a complex series of greys – some light, some dark. As I gazed out of the window looking down at the square and then up to the castle on the hill, it dawned on me that defending the peace could be just as important.

I decided to go to the nearest pub to celebrate over a pint and fell into conversation with an old soldier who convinced me that I was far better serving out my time in the service. He had heard that things outside were none too rosy. 'Thanks pal.' All I needed was reassurance. I left the pub with a new spring in my step and headed back to the barracks.